Dodging Elephants

By Alice Morrison

Here I am. Naked from the waist down, bent over, in a tent, with Ribka behind me wielding a torch and searching gingerly between my butt cheeks to check out the state of my saddle sores. This is not how I imagined it when I booked up for the Tour D'Afrique and launched into my full-scale fantasy of racing across Africa on my bike.

This is my story about that race and what it was like for a very ordinary person to race 12,000 kilometres across a very extraordinary continent.

Cover design and book formatting by Scot Kinkade,

scotkinkade@icloud.com

Edited by Tanya Woolf,

tanya@tanyawoolf.co.uk

The book is dedicated to my Mum and Dad, Fredi and Jim Morrison and my brother, Robbie Morrison.

It is also for the TDA family. I hope I did our story justice.

Chapter One

Egypt

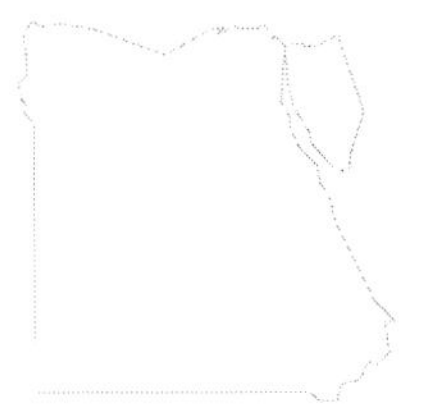

"Why, oh why, oh why?" It was day five of the great adventure. I had reached that breaking point when I was ready to admit that my Mother was right and I should never have, "left a great job in the middle of a recession to head off on a ridiculous fantasy where you will probably die and even if you don't you will ruin your life." My legs were ruined, my heart was pumping way too hard, I was breathing heavily and I had five hours left on the bike.

I had to ask myself what a not-very-sporty, middle aged woman with a deep love of cake and her sofa was doing perched on a custom-made bicycle, heading into the middle of Africa. "I am an Adventurer," I thought. "I can do this." Unfortunately, this didn't help much. The word "Adventurer" conjures up a vision in khaki, wearing one of those jackets with lots of pockets, probably with a beard, and definitely with a well-defined jaw and steely blue eyes. I was in a flowery lycra cycling top, with pigtails, sweating profusely, with red-rimmed eyes and absolutely no definition anywhere whatsoever.

We were going up a long, draggy hill out of Safaga on the Red Sea through the Sinai Desert. In order to make the distances, I was having to ride in a peloton with 9 other riders. When you are riding right in the middle of a well -defined peloton (main pack in a cycling race), the experts reckon you can save up to 40% of your energy as the other riders shelter you and create a tunnel through the air which makes it easier to ride through. It is also a good option because it makes you ride at a steady pace and you have the company of the other riders. The only problem with this one was that it was going about 5km per hour too fast for me. That meant that I was riding outside my comfort zone even with the shelter of the other riders. Psychologically, it is a very hard thing to get your head round, knowing that you are going to suffer not just for ten minutes or even half an hour, but all day and that day is going to be about six hours long. You have to concentrate every second to keep up and you have to stop yourself thinking, "I can't do this, I can't stand another five hours of this. I just can't cope." But I had to. I had 8000 miles still to go. It was just the beginning of the Tour D'Afrique

Adventures are like murder. All you really need is motive and opportunity and I had plenty of both spurring me on to race across Africa. My motive was a combination of a fascination for the continent and an urge to really try myself and see if I could conquer it. I was unfit, not young, not sporty and a bit of a softie, but I reckoned I could do it if I put my mind to it. I, probably foolishly, believed that all I needed was a bit of good, old-fashioned, British grit.

I blame my parents for this blithe, or perhaps blind, optimism. When I was six weeks old, and they were in their mid-twenties, we all set sail from Edinburgh for a new life in Uganda. They had taken up jobs as teachers and we were to stay there for the next eight years. When I think of it as an adult, and in our cautious age where children are so well protected and guarded, I blanch a bit. Dad had been a sailor in the merchant navy and had travelled a lot, but Mum hadn't. She had been brought up in Scotland, gone to Edinburgh University, and then packed her bags and headed for the Dark Continent with a tiny tot in tow. That takes real balls and I look back in admiration. I hope that that spirit of adventure was passed down to me. They certainly made everything feel possible, and in a very matter of fact way.

So, my first memory is not of the streets of Edinburgh but of an African warrior in full tribal dress, holding a spear, silhouetted against the dark of the open doorway, looking down on me. He must have been friendly because I have lived to tell this tale.

My brother and I grew up in the foothills of the Rwenzori mountains and we enjoyed an idyllic childhood. We ran free over the hills and through the shambas (subsistence farms) and banana plantations. We were always barefoot, spoke fluent Swahili, and hunted tadpoles in the huge puddles left by the rains. We lived above a game park and at weekends, Mum and Dad would take us down to drive through herds of elephant, zebra, buffalo and gazelles. It was beautiful but also frightening. Once, we were watching two young bucks fighting, when a lioness sprang from behind our car, which she had been using as a shield, and ripped the throat out of one of them. I can still see his death throes.

We had legions of pets including an owl, a tortoise, a pet goat, cats, and a dog called Haggis who was disgraced when he bit the tail off a sheep. We had to buy the sheep and watch it bleating pitifully in our garden until the gardener could dispatch it. Mum was so upset initially that she gave all the meat away, but then changed her mind when she saw the juiciness of the chops in question.

Joyous freedom was ours and nothing seemed impossible. Of course, bad things happened. One day I was out on a hike, aged around seven, with two of my friends and one of the Dads when we were attacked by a swarm of wild hornets. Terrified, screaming and in agony, the Dad yelled at us to head down for the river. We dunked ourselves in and stayed underwater till the hornets drowned or died. I had over a hundred stings on my head and my face swelled up like a balloon. Soon though, the pain was forgotten and it was one of our family stories with me as the heroine. An adventure. The seeds were sown.

At eight, my parents moved us all back to the west coast of Scotland, so that we could get a proper education. It was cold and wet and suddenly I was in a big school where nobody knew me. Unfortunately for me, I had been taught to read by my Mum and loved it and so could read better than anyone in the class. The teacher always picked me and I hated it. Why? Because I knew it quadrupled my chances of getting beaten up in the playground. Not only was I "Teacher's Pet", I had an English accent. I spent those first few months skulking in corners, with my head down, praying no-one would pick on me. It was a nightmare. But, the weeks wore on and I was adopted by a couple of kindred spirits and then there was fun to be had, making dens in the wood and venturing, shivering and quivering into the freezing North Sea.

Tour D'Afrique represented a chance to relive those childhood adventures and once again become the heroine of my own story. It was a powerful motive.

For my opportunity, I have to thank David Cameron and the Tory party. At the beginning of this story, my free African childhood was long behind me and I was suited (ish), booted and the Chief Executive of a Quango, Vision+Media. Our job was to develop the creative and media sector in the Northwest of England and it was a great job, working with a great team, and in a fantastic spot. Roll on the elections in May 2010. The day after the vote was announced, I went into the office and warned my team, that regardless of our success, we were entering a period of uncertainty. "Quangos are bad!" said the Tories with self-righteous indignation. "Regions are bad too." So, our funders were abolished and we merged into an England-wide entity.

It was a hideous time and horrible to see all the hard work we had been put in dismantled. Talented people were made redundant, and everyone had to suffer through months of uncertainty. Of course, I cared dreadfully and was furious. We were the most successful at what we did in the country, but that didn't matter, it was all about a press headline for the new government. I knew that the infrastructure that was being dismantled at huge cost in terms of tax payer money for redundancy, fulfilment of contracts and so on, would all be re-instated in new forms, and of course it was. The government spent even more money setting up even more bodies.

But, we had to accept it, rescue what we could and build for the future. And it gave me my opportunity.

Opportunity and also a visceral need to get away from all the bullshit. I was enraged and disgusted by what had happened. I was searching for something totally different and I found it in the Tour D'Afrique.

I had been looking for biking holidays in Africa about three years before with my friend Karina, when the Tour D'Afrique (TDA) popped up. "You can do it, "she said. "It's long but you'll make it. You're not fast but you're steady and you can keep going for ages." I kept it in my head as something I wanted to do and would go back to it from time to time and do a little day dreaming. That dreaming turned into a reality and I signed up in November for the start at the beginning of January, so it was going to be a kick,bollock, scramble to get ready.

The Tour D'Afrique is the longest bike race in the world. It runs annually, starting in Cairo in January and ending in Cape Town in May. It is 12,000 kilometres long and crosses 10 countries: Egypt, Sudan, Ethiopia, Kenya, Tanzania, Malawi, Zambia, Botswana, Namibia and South Africa. It is three and a bit times as long as the Tour De France. The racing format is that of a stage race and there are 100 stages varying from 40 km to 200 km. There are about 20 rest days. The 2003 Tour D'Afrique set a Guinness World Record for the fastest crossing of Africa by bicycle and this was achieved by nine participants of the race. The roads are a mixture of tarmac and dirt and the condition of them varies widely. The terrain covers everything: mountains, deserts, jungle, plains and forest.

It is run by a Toronto-based company, owned by Henry Gold, one of the original riders. The Tour is fully-supported so that competitors only have to carry what they need for the day on their bikes, and there is also a lunch stop and water refill. There are four support vehicles: Two trucks to transport all the riders' kit, including tents, bike spares and everything else you can think of, one medical van which doubles up as the lunch truck and the Tour Leader's vehicle which is also used for emergency pick-ups and scouting.

Sixty-three of us were full competitors for the race, eleven women and fifty-two men and we were joined by various people to do sections and stages. From the brave sixty-three there were a hard core of racers who had come, not just for the adventure of crossing Africa, but also for the race itself, and then the rest were what the TDA team call Expedition Riders. I was one of these, seduced by the blurb which describes an Expedition Rider like this, "They cover each day at their own pace, stopping in the villages and roadside cafes....." HA! Little did I know.

November and two months till I started. The minute I signed up I started to worry about everything – money, fitness, kit, bike, tent and and and. I had eight weeks to go, it was the middle of a nasty, snowy winter and I had nothing sorted. Many sleepless nights ensued. As it was to turn out, that mattered for some things but not for others. The thing it mattered most for, though, was bike fitness. I was in reasonably good nick in terms of fitness having got my weight down to around 10 ½ stone and exercising about five times a week for the past year. But I was in no way bike fit. I have always loved biking and can still remember the day my stabilisers came off. I am a leisure biker but have done a few longer trips of a couple of weeks here and there in various far flung places, but nothing like this. I would mountain bike round Hayfield in the Peak District most weekends and I had a set of rollers at home so I could bike in my sitting room while watching Strictly Come Dancing but this was really not enough, and I was to suffer for it when we started. Really suffer.

The two major things I had to sort out were my kit and my bike. The bike was going to be welded to my backside for nearly five months so it was really important that I get it right and this is where Dave rode to the rescue. He is a professional bike-man, working for a giant bicycle manufacturer (yes, the clue is in the description) and he became my very own bike builder. I didn't realise how very little I knew about bikes until Dave started asking me questions.

"So, Alice, do you want to race or to ride?"

"Ride! I want to get through it which I think is going to be hard enough." That one was easy. What it meant for Dave was that he ruled out a cyclocross bike which would have gone faster but would have been a much less comfortable ride. Almost all the racers were on some form of cyclocross. So, I was going to have a mountain bike.

"How much of the journey is on pavement and how much on dirt track and would you rather go faster on the pavement or be more comfortable on the dirt?"

"I think it is about 60/40 and I want it to be do-able on the dirt but not too mountain-bike sticky-wheels on the pavement because that is really knackering." This meant I ended up with a steel frame, an On One Inbred, which has more give in it and so is a little more forgiving over the ruts. Carbon frames were more or less banned as if they break there was nowhere to fix them and the rules of the Tour state that you have to start and finish on the same bike. If my steel frame had broken, any blacksmith along the way could have mended it. Tyres were the other really important factor. I ended up with Kojak slicks for the road which were amazing. They had no tread at all, so I could go like the clappers, well downhill anyway. For off-road we chose two different treads, one of which worked and one of which didn't, but more of that later. The third thing to consider for comfort was suspension. Suspension cushions you but it both slows you down and uses up more energy to ride, neither of which I could really afford. Back suspension was out of the question as it takes too much energy but I did want suspension on my front fork. Dave went for Rock Shocks which have an excellent lock off facility. This means you can make the front fork rigid when you are on the road and soft when you are off-road.

"What kind of bike position do you want to have?"

This threw me a bit as I wasn't sure. I wanted to be able to look around but also minimise back pain and optimise leg efficiency. We settled on a sit up and beg and Dave gave me a shorter frame than I am used to so that I would be in a strongly upright position.

"Do you want to take panniers or are you going to carry everything on your back?"

"On my back, I am used to it from mountain biking and I like to have my water in my camelback so I can drink all the time." I didn't even think about this as I was so sure that it would be the best option. That hasty answer returned to haunt me.

The bike component manufacturer, SRAM, supplied all my gearing, derailleur and disc brakes. Dave chose for durability and reliability on everything. Then he built my wonderful bike, my best friend for the months and kilometres to come.

Over the next few weeks, I got my kit together as per the list that the TDA team had supplied us all with. I stuck to it rigidly. Well, almost, I did pack a dress and some earrings and Chanel red lipstick. My tent arrived mid-December; I splurged out a ridiculous amount of money on the most expensive cycling shorts in Europe; I got out and cleaned all my existing equipment and by Christmas I had everything ready.

On the 27th December, I handed over the keys of my house to my new tenants, said goodbye to the cats, who were largely unmoved, and got in the car to drive up to Edinburgh where I was going to spend the last week at my parents' before heading off. I would miss the rest of winter and the whole of spring and by the time I got back, I would have cycled across a continent. It all felt unreal. The next week passed in a blur of last minute buys and preparations, Mum's cooking and then the airport drop-off with Dad and my brother, Robbie, hefting the luggage and bikes and I was on my way.

" This is not so much a race as a social experiment." That was our introduction to the Tour from Sharita Van der Merwe our scary, but fabulous, tour leader. She was to rule her crew, and us, with a rod of iron and could reduce the strongest of men to a quivering heap with just a glance. Exactly what you want when you are about to set off across a big, unstable continent.

All 63 of us had congregated in the ballroom of our hotel near the Pyramids for our first full briefing. Meeting any big group of new people is pretty intimidating, but meeting a group of hard-core, type A, super-fit, super-competitive, mainly male, kitted up cyclists is terrifying. Much later, I discovered that I wasn't the only person who had been intimidated. Ribka and Aman, a married couple from Ethiopia and Eritrea, were moving to South Africa from the US to start a new life in Africa and had the brilliant idea of cycling there rather than just catching a plane. Neither of them were dedicated cyclists.

"So, Alice," Ribka told me, "We looked around the room to see if there was anyone we could team up with. We knew we were going to be really slow and at the back and we were hoping that we could meet up with some other people who would be more on our level. There were way too many muscled calves and people talking about racing for our liking. Then we spotted a really beautiful older woman and her husband and we thought great, they're older so they'll be a bit slower like us. We headed over and buddied up with them. In our room that night we did a bit of self congratulation on our cleverness, thinking we were set."

The only problem with this was that they had chosen Christine and Paul – and Paul, a world champion rider, went on to win the whole race.

We were to have rider meetings every day that we were on the road. They happened just before supper and we were told what lay ahead the next day, went through the route, any hazards, news and country information. The first one was dedicated to explaining to us the various ways that we might die or injure ourselves along the way. These ranged from being bitten by venomous snakes you may have found on the road and decided to stroke, to drowning in your own vomit after a serious crash. We were also introduced to the crew members who would be looking after us. They were all young and adventurous and, like the riders, from all over the world. We had James and Kim cooking, Martin and Gabe mechanicking, Claire looking after us medically, Christiano on Communications, Nick directing the race and Elvis riding with us and helping out. There were also local drivers and guides who changed throughout the tour.

Our first set of snack bars and our timing chips were handed out, and we had to bring our bags to be weighed and measured so that the crew could check they would fit in the lockers. We also got our directions for the first day's riding. Setting off from the hotel and the official launch of the race from the Pyramids. It was all getting a bit real, I thought, as I set off back to my hotel room. There, I had my first encounter with Ruth.

"Oh hullo," she said brusquely, "You're my roommate. I hate sharing rooms. I don't know why we have to. I tried to get my own. I'm Ruth."

The very first day. We had a pre-dawn start from the hotel to get us up to the pyramids for our official launch. I think everyone was nervous because no matter how good and confident a biker you were, we were going out into the unknown. There was lots of noise and chat, laughter and scoping out of everyone else's bikes, kit and muscles. I had that slightly pleasurable sick nerves feeling and was worrying generically about keeping up, navigating a big biking group, cycling through the Cairo traffic, and wondering whether the BBC news camera woman and I would actually manage to meet up at the pyramids. Then we were off, off on our big adventure. 134 kms to cover. From Cairo to the desert and the night's camp, and the first rest day a long way off on day seven. We unfurled in a long banner of lycra up to the pyramids and round the back. Cycling through the pyramids at dawn is magical. Cairo is just starting to wake up and you are wending your way up with the first few camels and tourist touts. We stopped at the point where you can see all three pyramids with the city in the background. A little stage had been set up and some tea and cakes. It didn't feel like we deserved them as we had only cycled a couple of kilometres, but we tucked in anyway. There were lots of local news crews and brief speeches. Back on the bikes and down past the sphinx. I felt like I was going to burst with excitement, I was on a bike, in Cairo, at the pyramids, with a whole continent ahead of me.

If you've been to Cairo, you will know that the traffic is horrific and you take your life in your hands every time you step into a taxi. Men do use bikes there, but it would be impossible for a woman to cycle alone. We had a police escort and our convoy of trucks to protect us, and kept in tight formation as we navigated over the flyovers and down the dual carriageways. The Cairenes were enthusiastic supporters - no horn was left unhonked. People clapped and cheered by the side of the road and shouted, "Shiddee Haylak" (Be strong!) from their car windows. The main difficulty was making sure you didn't crash into the bikers in front of you as the convoy slowed down and speeded up along the route, the other problem was that having drunk lots of tea and juice, I was dying for a wee after about an hour and there was absolutely nowhere for us to go, in the most densely populated city in Africa. The boys just pulled over to the side of the road or dodged under one of the flyover bridges, but there was no chance of that for the women, so we just had to clench those pelvic floors and ride it out, till we found a blessed petrol station at the very outskirts of the city.

Once we left Cairo behind us, we got onto the desert highway and headed out on a long, straight, flat road that was to take us to the Sinai. The traffic was light, mainly lorries, and they gave us a wide berth. The weather was cool and misty and the road surface was good so it was a great introduction and a chance to calm down and get the nerves under control, after the excitement of the send off. The rest of the ride went smoothly. Not much to look at because we were basically going down a big arterial dual carriage way but conversations with other riders and the first set of character judgements to make; so many of which inevitably proved totally wrong. It was a bit like your first day at secondary school.

The hardest part was actually after the ride had finished, as this was when I had to finally grapple with how to put my tent up. A sensible person would have tackled this long before and practised at home, but a fear of instruction booklets and the snowiest winter we had had for several years, prevented me from taking that logical step. So, with the rider meeting and then supper beckoning, I pulled my monster out of its bag and faced it. That tent was to prove my nemesis. I had chosen it because it was a really good brand from an (allegedly) really good shop and from my online research it had looked great. The best thing was that it had room to stand up in, and I thought this would be perfect for when I was washing with wet wipes and also sorting out my saddle sores. I was, in fact, proud of my foresight and planning. What I hadn't considered was that the tent was shaped like a sail, and so took off at any breath of wind. What's more, it had a pole and guy rope system impenetrable to modern woman. Add that to my technical incompetence and you get nightly disaster. Once I had pulled it all out of its bag, I looked at it, pulled out the biggest pole you have ever seen and realised that I had absolutely no idea where to even start. Sam and Stephen to my undying gratitude came to the rescue. The three of us struggled through and three quarters of an hour later, the thing was up, well up enough anyway. Frazzled and grateful, I got through the first supper and then to bed. And really that first day was to be a microcosm of the whole trip. There were going to be fantastic moments, uncomfortable moments, humiliating moments, peaceful moments and through all of them an unflinching camaraderie.

The next day was a Mando day, mando being short for mandatory. In each section of the Tour, there was at least one mandatory day, which meant that the racers had to complete it or be disqualified from the race. What it also meant was that it was the hardest day of that section. Oblivious to this, I woke up feeling perky, not too stiff, and ready to go.

"I can do this," I thought, as God laughed quietly to himself.

Eleven hours later, as the last glimmer of light faded, I and a dozen others were swept up by the support truck, just 10km short of home. The rule was that if you hadn't made camp by dark, the truck would come and get you. I was gutted. Swept up on day two. I had tried my hardest and I had failed. What I hadn't appreciated was the effect of a strong headwind on your speed. That stretch is notorious for it, and it hadn't disappointed. It kept up for the whole day and just to help, kicked in more strongly after lunch. There is virtually nothing more dispiriting than cycling into a headwind, it saps all your energy both physical and mental. More experienced riders had joined up and ridden in pelotons to save their strength. I had teamed up with Mike with no bike but two people do not a peloton make. Mike with no bike, was a young American entrepreneur who had had a really fancy bike built for the Tour. But it hadn't arrived and in spite of dozens of increasingly frantic calls to the airline it was still missing in action when we set off. So, he was on a bike that he had bought in Cairo which I can exclusively reveal was not at all fancy. He was really good humoured about it, but it must have made things really difficult. That bike never did arrive but Mike ordered a new one which arrived after Ethiopia, and then he was known as Mike with two bikes.

As so often happens though, something great came out of that second day's failure. Standing by the road where we got swept up was a slim, snowy-bearded, German cyclist also called Mike and German Mike was to be my riding buddy from that day on.

The next day we joined a peloton. No more "I can do this" thoughts from me. I had switched to, "How am I going to survive this." Mike and I scouted around at dinner and breakfast and then hooked ourselves onto a group that seemed round about the right level. It was run with ruthless efficiency by Peter Prins. There were ten of us and we cycled in pairs. We took 5 km stints at the front, which was probably a bit too long but also meant you had a longer respite and we stopped every hour or 25 kms for just long enough to have a pee and a banana. Lunch break was about 45 mins. I had to struggle to keep up and fight hard when I was at the front, but it meant that I knew I would do the distance, and that was the really important thing. The good thing about being in a peloton, apart from the energy saving, is that you have company which helps the miles to go. It was a quick way to get to know people a bit better and get more comfortable in the group. We could imprint a mini team identity within the larger mass of riders.

"Alice, Alice," I was lying in my tent, earplugs in, head zipped into the hood of my sleeping bag, trying to block out the world for a few hours and pretend I wasn't really doing this, but I could hear Ruth and she was being very insistent.

"Alice, Alice. Get up. Your tent is blowing down. Hurry up. It's about to collapse. Get up. Get up." I unzipped and looked into the maelstrom. The sides of my tent were banging together with the force of the wind, and everything was swaying wildly. There was a massive banging and clunking noise as the poles and ropes jostled together. I shot out of the door and there was Ruth, hanging on for dear life to two of my guy ropes as my tent made a concerted bid to fly out over the Red Sea. I grabbed another couple of guy ropes and we clung on. There was activity all around us as campers re-pegged their tents to try and keep them stable in the storm. A pop up tent somersaulted past us, pursued by a semi-clad rider. I knew I had no chance whatsoever. I had a tent that could have powered a catamaran and there weren't enough tent pegs in the world to make it secure in the sandy soil. So, we dragged my stuff out, collapsed the tent, and stuffed it into its bag. Two Egyptian men came up and helped us gather my scattered belongings and said they would store it for me, so I gave it up gratefully.

"Do you know them? " asked Ruth, two minutes later.

"No, but I am sure they're with the crew, aren't they?" I was too miserable and confused to care really. I was standing in a sandstorm in my pyjamas, needing desperately to sleep so I could cope with the next day, and I had no tent. And that is when Ruth, the woman who "doesn't like sharing hotel rooms" showed her true colours.

"Come in with me, we'll just peg the tent down a bit more." I could have kissed her. We were both dirty, smelly and tired but she was willing to give up half the space in her two-man tent to me, just four days after we had met. In fact, it was really nice to bunk in together and have a laugh about the storm, the hard days on the bike and the strangeness of it all. I slept really well, only vaguely troubled by the fact that I may have given all my kit into the hands of a couple of complete strangers and never see it again.

I did of course. It was there, waiting in one of the lorries for me the next morning. Everyone had a story to tell about the storm, but they were unanimous in voting my tent the most ridiculous and impractical edifice ever seen in Africa.

The first few days had passed in a kind of dream. There was so much to get used to. I was really glad we were in Egypt. I had lived in Cairo for two years when I left university, and because I had studied Arabic, I had a massive advantage in terms of language and culture. It was a really comfortable start for me. The things that many of the other riders found strange about being in an Islamic and Arab culture were familiar and welcoming. What wasn't familiar or welcoming was almost everything else. Human nature being what it is, I assumed that everyone had got the hang of things and it was just me who still couldn't work out the daily routines and rules: how to stuff everything into my locker, where to wash my hands before meals, how to get into the food queue before the ravenous boys, how to bag a seat before the grandfather's club had grabbed all of them, how to put up my tent - actually that last one was just me and I never really conquered it.

After the first few days, I was able to start looking around me. The scenery was stark but with a clear, golden light dancing over the sand. We were right in the middle of the Sinai desert with its clean sand and rolling hills. The roads were paved and smooth with very little traffic and you could see for miles. After the horror of the mando day, the headwind had also dropped and it was a perfect temperature, sunny but cool. We were flanked by the Red Sea and the play of light changed throughout the day. I was also beginning to get to know people a little, and to work better in the peloton, so things were easing up. But my lack of bike fitness was really killing. When I had spoken to the TDA crew before I came they had reassured me that it really wouldn't matter too much and that I could train in as we crossed Egypt. They were right in that the biking was doable, but it hurt and it made the first fortnight physically miserable. Cycling in the peloton above my comfortable speed meant that I couldn't relax at all. I had to be mentally present all the time. Time for some mind games.

"It's only 25kms till our first stop. I can do this. If I can keep going for 5 kms at the front, then the hard work will be done and I can relax for the next 20 kms because I'll be sheltered. I'm fine. I can do it. In 15 minutes we'll be stopping for a quick rest and I can uncramp my back. I think I am stronger than yesterday." What I couldn't afford to do was think further ahead. This was very difficult but crucial. My mind would start to stray.

"I've got 6 more hours of this today. I've got 134 kms left to go. Then I've got to put my tent up, have supper, sort out my kit, sleep and then do it all again tomorrow and the day after." I had to shut down those thoughts because they made it unbearable. It was just too big and everything was hurting. Because I hadn't trained properly and spent enough hours in the saddle, my body was having to toughen up as we went, with no time for respite or recovery. In order of pain this is how it felt.

My back from my neck down to the middle of my shoulders was in spasm. I felt like a red hot poker had been shoved down my cycling shirt and it burnt with increasing intensity throughout the day. I couldn't rotate my head properly and looking over my shoulder was just not an option. This was because I was carrying a heavy pack which dragged on me. I had opted not to have panniers but to carry my water and day's supplies on my back. I reckon it weighed around 8 kgs which doesn't sound like much but felt like a ton. Most of the weight was down to water. I carried two litres in my camelbak and a further one and a half in bottles. I always drink a lot on the bike and was paranoid about running out. Apart from that, I had spare inner tubes, pump, sun tan cream, a cover up top, snacks, money, a camera and a notebook and pen. My lower back got a bit stiff but wasn't too bad at the beginning. Sitting on the saddle for so many hours a day meant I had a sore seat. I didn't develop any saddle sores at the very beginning, but that first ten minutes in the morning when I swung my leg over the bar and then sat down, were excruciating. My thighs were achy, sometimes cramping up a bit towards the end of the day, but more of an overall dull pain. We were helped in that there weren't too many big climbs, and the road surface was smooth so we weren't bashed around. But how I wished I had trained and hardened up before I came. I think I would still have hurt, just because of the sheer volume of riding but I would definitely have hurt a lot less. One good thing about the pain though, was when we got off the bikes at the end of the day and it stopped, it felt exquisite. Lying or sitting down on even the most uncomfortable surface and knowing that I didn't have to bike for at least 12 hours and that the pain was over for the day was heaven. And it is quite hard to actually describe the joy and relief of zipping up my crazy tent and climbing into my sleeping bag with all my tasks finished and a whole ten hours of rest to look forward to.

We left the Sinai behind and turned in to the canals and tributaries of the Nile, and the great river itself. The Nile was to be with us for a long way, all the way down through the rest of Egypt and then into the Sudan, reappearing in Ethiopia. We arrived in the historic city of Luxor, famous for the Valley of the Kings and the temple of Karnak, relics of the magnificence of the Pharaohs, and plonked ourselves in a hotel and camp site at the edge of town. Hardy souls pitched their tents, but the lure of a real bed, a shower and toilet had me running for a hotel room. Marelie Van Der Merwe and I shared a room and we were to become roommates on the rest days for the next couple of months. She was a South African, living in Ghana, and had decided to do the Tour mainly on her own, but with Deon, her husband, coming to join her a little further down the race. The hotel was pretty grotty but there was good food in the cafe downstairs and lots of room to clean and footle with our bikes. Luxor is a beautiful town, facing on to the Nile and with Karnak as a dazzling centre piece. Because I had been so often when I lived in Egypt, I didn't feel any pressure to sightsee, so spent my time mooching around and chatting to people and relaxing, though I couldn't resist a felucca (sailboat) ride at sunset. The boys made their way as one to the nearest McDonalds, sometimes you crave the comforts of home.

That Friday, I noticed that the mosques were busy and that the sermons were longer than normal but thought nothing of it. Everywhere seemed calm and peaceful. I had absolutely no inkling that ten days later the Arab Spring was going to sweep across Egypt and that within the month, Hosni Mubarak who had been in power since I lived there 28 years before, would be toppled by a mass uprising. In retrospect, I wonder if I had been so focussed on the biking and the surviving, that I had my eyes and ears closed to what was going on. I talked to lots of Egyptians in Cairo and in Luxor and asked how business and the economy was. Everyone gave the answers that you would expect. Things were going pretty well and the tourist season was not bad but the roads needed fixed and government wages weren't high enough. I got told the same jokes about Hosni Mubarak and donkeys that had been doing the rounds for years and got the same complaints about how expensive it was to get married. I had also marked, particularly in Cairo, the lack of development and progress in the country. The roads were a mess, the flats still looked like they were half finished or about to fall down, the streets were filthy and overcrowded and the shops were much the same as they always had been. But I honestly got no sense that within days the country would be in full revolt and that the demonstrations in Tahrir would be changing history.

Luxor was our first rest day. The hotel may have been grotty but after 7 days of riding it was blissful not to be on the bike and to have a whole day to myself, and also not to have to struggle putting up the tent. There were a lot of tasks to do. I had to do my washing, clean and oil my bike, check and repack all my kit now I had a slightly better idea of what I was going to use, write my blog and catch up with everyone at home. At this stage in the game, I had lots of energy, so I did all my bits and pieces and still found plenty of time to go down to the suqs (markets) and have coffee and chat with people. I love Egypt. The other Arabs all say of the Egyptians, "Dammahum Khafif' which literally means that they have "light blood". And as much as you can generalise about any group of people they are indeed light hearted and have a great sense of humour, in fact a sense of humour that is not too far from the British one. Because I speak Arabic, I do get those bonus brownie points from a people that are already naturally friendly and hospitable. So, that first rest day didn't only soothe the body but soothed the soul as well.

What's more we had two easy-ish stages ahead of us and then two days on a boat as we sailed across Lake Nasser into the Sudan. Two days was a lot easier to face than seven days. And we were also going through Edfu and Aswan, which are nice towns. Edfu is a typical southern Egypt town with both Nubian and Arab populations which gives you hints of the Africa to come. When we got there we were camped in a big school sports field on the edge of the town. I arrived in time to go for a little explore of the town and a wander through the vegetable market. Tomatoes look very different from how they look on our Tesco shelves at home, but no matter how misshapen they are, the sun means that they taste sweet and delicious. I ambled around with the two Kims and Pretty Peter, so-called because he is gorgeous, and we stopped for Arabic coffee at a little café and watched the world go by. Peter and young Kim had bonded on day one and were to become best friends on the tour, riding together for much of the way, brothers of the bike. It was a nice relaxed end to the day, and more in keeping with how I had imagined TDA would be. That night though ended up being one of my nights of great shame.

The time has come to talk of toilets. As you would imagine on a trip like this, toilets are a big deal, especially for the women. I don't often get penis envy but this was one of those times. I was drinking an average of four litres of water a day on the bike and eating between 4000 and 6000 calories so that all had to get processed out. While we were in the Sinai, it hadn't been too bad. We could nip behind a dune and have a pee, and as there were so few people and so little traffic, it wasn't much of a problem. You did have to make a decision which way to face to the road – face forward so other riders could see your face but not your bottom, or the other way. Psychologically, I decided that if I couldn't see them, then they couldn't see me, so a lot of riders got way too many views of my bared arse. But when we got to the more populated areas of Luxor, Edfu and Aswan, it all became a lot more difficult. We were cycling beside the Nile and the Nile canals, and the whole area is intensively farmed. There are people everywhere. If you saw a likely spot, you had to leap off the bike and whip down your sweaty shorts as quickly as you could, while squatting on those aching thighs. When we were in camp in this early part of the tour, there were toilets on site. But they just could not compete with the volume. Also, the staff didn't tell everyone that in Egypt you don't put toilet paper down the toilet but in a bin because the drains can't take it. Add to this the fact that by this stage almost everyone had a bad stomach, and the toilets were blocked and unbearable within about an hour of being in camp. So, on to my night of shame. We had dinner as usual at around six before the sun went down. Some of the kids from the school where we were camped had come down and there was an impromptu game of football. I watched for a bit and then I headed off to my tent which I had pitched in the middle of the group. I fell asleep listening to the muezzin at one of the three mosques which surrounded us and all was well. About two in the morning, I woke up with bad stomach cramps. I tried to ignore them because I knew how rank the toilets were and it was dark, but to no avail, I had to go, and go quickly. I scrambled out the tent in my pyjamas, with my head torch and headed off to where the toilet block was. But it wasn't there and by this time things were becoming urgent. I hobbled round the perimeter, searching for the toilets, and still couldn't find them. My head torch wasn't helping much in the pitch black and by now I was doubled over. Crisis point was reached, I staggered to the nearest dark corner, switched off the head torch and off I went. I was there for about five minutes and it was not a happy experience. All I could think was, "Those poor school kids, I am shitting on their playground!"

Aswan was our last stop in Egypt and came at the end of another beautiful day cycling by the Nile. The river is flanked on either side by rich, green fields, dotted with palms and two storey red mud houses. This lushness comes to an abrupt end where the irrigation channels stop and then you have the desert rising all around. It is the contrast that makes it so remarkable and there is always something to look at. The white-sailed feluccas on the water, the overladen donkey carts taking the vegetables to the market and the old men in galabeyyas (long robes) sitting by the road smoking shisha. The other memorable thing about that part of the journey was the falafel. Deep fried balls made of green beans, stuffed in pitta bread with chilli sauce and slathered in a thin yoghurt. Our crew had commandeered a falafel seller for our lunch stop, he was cooking at break neck speed to keep up with us and crowds of people had gathered to watch, including the entire girls' primary school opposite who were desperate to talk to these weird people who had landed in their midst. They all wanted to have their picture taken and were fighting to hold our hands and get in the middle. We were to find that almost the whole way down. Ethiopia was to be a bit of an exception.

Two days on a boat, crossing the huge expanse of water that is Lake Nasser, heading towards the Sudan. Lake Nasser is Egypt and partially Sudan's water storage. It was created when the Nile was blocked by the Aswan High Dam, and now the seasonal floods of the river are controlled to stop the catastrophic flood and drought that used to affect Egypt so regularly. Getting onto the ferry, which we shared with sharp-elbowed Sudanese, livestock and every kind of manufactured good, was worse than Black Friday in an electrical store. Territory was marked out on deck and small makeshift tents erected.

Luckily for me, lots of our group suffered from seasickness and wanted to be out in the open, so I got a cabin and snored my way through the voyage.

Chapter Two

Sudan

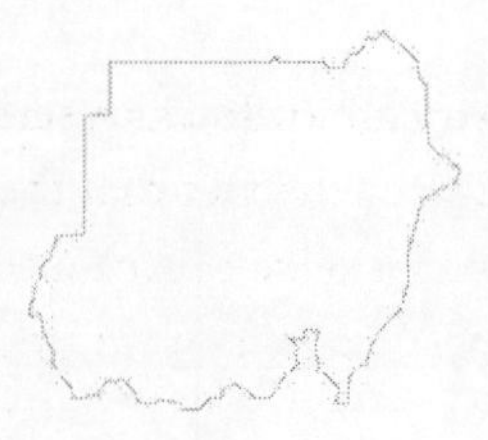

My favourite story about the Sudan, didn't actually happen to me, it happened to our oldest competitor, Bob. Bob is a real English gent, even though he has spent half a lifetime in Australia and claims Ozzie nationality. He was in his late sixties at the time of the Tour and really wiry and fit. He was always charming and a pleasure to be around, although, like all of us he had his foibles. His particular foible was a penchant for public nudity. I am still scarred by the memory of flinging open my tent flap one evening in Kenya to be confronted by Bob full frontal bathing in a very small bucket of water. But back to the story. It was one of the really, really hot days in the Sudan when the temperature went over 50 degrees. Not surprisingly, there was no water for washing or cooling down in, as we had to save all the supplies for drinking. After 150 kms in the saddle in those temperatures, you were desperate to get some water on your skin. We were roughly following the Nile at this stage but were not close enough to get in it. On this particular day, just at the end of the ride, there was a small, muddy canal. Bob had spotted this, and when he got there, chucked his bike onto the bank, pulled off his biking shoes and went straight in. Imagine the pleasure. Bob wallowed like a water buffalo and brought his temperature down to, if not cool, at least tepid. Then after half an hour, he got up to go on to the camp a couple of kilometres away, but he had to climb up the muddy bank to get back to his bike. All this time, a man had been watching him, and he beckoned to Bob to go with him. Bob picked up his shoes and went. The man spoke no English, and Bob no Arabic, so Bob wondered what was in store for him. When they got to his house, the man sat him down, brought a basin of clean water and washed and dried his feet. He hadn't wanted Bob to put his shoes on while they were muddy. Of all the wonderful people we met on our trip, the Sudanese, were the kindest and the most hospitable.

Before we had left the UK, one of the time consuming and difficult parts of the preparation was to get our Sudanese visas. We had to get them before we left as there was no chance of getting them en route. Right up until we set sail on Lake Nasser, we were not sure that we would be able to go through the

Sudan at all. The state of semi-warfare in the North was a serious consideration for the TDA organisers, as was the fact that the referendum on independence for the South of the Sudan had taken place just before we got there, and the results were due to be announced while we were still in the country. What the TDA crew could not have predicted is that in the two days that we sailed across Lake Nasser, revolution was breaking out in the country we had just left behind. For our whole journey through Sudan, I would stop at every roadside cafe, or barber shop, or hotel that had satellite TV to try and see what was happening as the Arab Spring raged through Egypt. Interestingly, almost all were tuned to BBC Arabic TV, and almost none to Al Jazeera. This was really gratifying to me as I had worked at BBC Arabic TV and am a believer in the BBC's integrity. When I asked why they preferred the BBC, the answer was always the same - Al Jazeera has a political agenda and the BBC doesn't.

Our own personal taste of mass violence had been the struggle to get on the ferry for our trip across the Lake and now we were in our second country. The first three days riding when we got into the Sudan were a bit similar to what we had just come from in the Sinai but more pristine and beautiful. Long, straight roads with sand mountains and hills flanking us. The light glowed, especially in the morning and the late afternoon and the tarmac was immaculate. There was almost no traffic at all, except for a couple of columns of tanks moving north, presumably to keep a wary eye on the border as Egypt convulsed. These were good days. We were still riding in the peloton but I felt more confident, stronger in my legs and back after a couple of weeks on the bike and even more importantly, I was starting to feel better in my head. I wasn't worried every day that I wouldn't be able to finish or that I wouldn't be able to put my tent up. I had started to make friends and get comfortable. Routine is a very comforting thing and that had kicked in. I could feel my head emptying of everything except for the journey. The heat was rising but manageable and we only had three days riding to our first rest day of Dongola. On the day riding in to Dongola I wrote in my diary, "felt comfortable for the first time on the bike." It had only taken eleven stages to get there and of course, it wasn't to last.

Dongola is actually a big centre by Sudanese standards but to us it felt like a really small town. It had a good campsite and a couple of hotels and a main street with a variety of shops in it, including food shops that stocked delicacies for us – fresh cheese and yoghurt. It also had the all-important telecom shop so that we could get our local SIM cards. These were vital on the trip and one of the first things we did in each country was get a local card. Mobile coverage right across Africa is pretty good and cheap as long as you are not using your European/US/home sim. For all my rest days, I had decided early on to stay in hotels if at all possible. My tent and I were still not friends, so me and the Grandad club all booked in to a small guest house which boasted hot (ish) showers and satellite TV. The Grandad club was actually a bit of a misnomer as not all the members had grandkids but was coined as a generic phrase for some of our older guys. All of whom, were strong and fit and fast. They were also demanding, and I spent most of that first rest day sorting out sims and also sourcing somewhere to eat. It is great speaking the language, but it also ends up imposing a few duties on you.

Dongola was relaxing and relaxed, a great place for a rest day when it was all about cleaning yourself, your bike and your kit and eating as much good food as possible. In this case, delicious falafel and then outstanding grilled chicken, whole ones, and chips. The grilled chicken place was huge and open with benches outside. It was really popular with queues of Sudanese waiting for their takeaways and TDAers dominating the tables. It was warm and noisy with Arabic music competing with the laughter and banter. The various types of chicken and meat were barbecued or grilled on enormous kebab turner, so that the smoke and the smell wafted over to the hungry diners all waiting with forks poised. It was to be a constantly repeated phenomenon that when TDA rolled into town, we would find with laser-like speed the best places to eat and then all descend like a big crowd of locusts. We were our own economic boom, as we cleaned shops out of snacks and restaurants out of whatever they were serving.

That night in the hotel, was very strange. The hotel was very basic and not very clean. It also played home to lots of mosquitoes and a few cockroaches. But it was a bed, and I was determined to get a good night's sleep before getting back on the bike. This was not to be. At around midnight, a woman started wailing and screaming. I didn't know what it was, so I got dressed and went outside to the courtyard but couldn't see anything. It sounded like a mixture between pain and ecstasy and was both loud and eerie. I could hear an intermittent male voice trying to soothe but she went on and on and on for another three hours. In the morning, as we were leaving, we got an abashed apology from the owner of the hotel. Apparently he and his wife had been enjoying their conjugals. I almost wished I had stayed in my tent.

Dongola to Dead Camel Camp was our next stage. And yes the clue is in the title, our camp had a dead camel in the middle of it which Kristian, one of our youngest riders and a great photographer, decided to pitch his tent near to. Our route lay along the caravan trail and so was littered with the skeletons and remains of camels which hadn't made it from the south. Camels are still widely used as pack animals and for transport. They are more reliable and use less energy than a 4x4, and the caravan routes from southern Africa up through the deserts to the North continue to be travelled as they have for hundreds of years. The riding for these next four days was really good. I definitely felt a lot stronger and even rode with the faster group for a couple of days. Our average speed was kicking up to 30kms an hour and I wasn't suffering. Each riding day was around 145 kms which was right on our average for the tour and manageable. My legs still hurt at the end of the day but I didn't feel like I was hanging on for dear life to stay with the group. The temperatures stayed good in the 30s and early 40s and we still had nice roads and clear desert views. The Nile was constantly on our right hand side, a constant strip of green cultivation with tiny villages, just clusters of low red mud brick buildings strung along it.

Dead Camel Camp was right beside the Nile. A big sand dune and some trekking through fields and then you were there. After a day's riding and then the nightly struggle with my tent, I was a hot, sweaty mess and the thought of cooling off was irresistible. Resolutely pushing all thoughts of Bilharzia from my mind, I got my swimsuit on, grabbed my soap and towel and trudged on down. What do you imagine when you think of swimming in the Nile? Cool, clear water, waving palm trees and perhaps a decorative child or two on the bank. The reality is a sludgy green, brown river shared with donkeys and cows and many, many biting insects. Everyone else was in though, so I was going too, even if it looked entirely unappealing. Once I was in past the mud it was cool and soft and soothing for the legs and bottom. Floating weightlessly but making sure not to get too far downstream as the current was strong, I soaped away and tried not to think about the donkey poo floating past.

As we were waiting for supper, Dennis provided our evening's entertainment. Dennis was one of our racing stars and a bit of a comedian on the side. Originally from Germany, but living in Switzerland, we cycled at very different rates but shared a common love of chocolate. On this evening, he had headed off to the desert for his ablutions, carrying the toilet shovel and some paper. It was an idyllic scene, the sun was bathing the sky in pink, there were the noises of cooking from the camp and a group of local boys and their camels were wandering picturesquely through the tents. He found a large and discreet hummock at a reasonable distance away and proceeded. Moments later, there was a yell and some frantic and bare-arsed activity. One of the camels had decided to take a much, much closer look at what this strange beast was up to, and Dennis was flushed from his hiding place, running and screaming like a banshee and wielding the toilet shovel to no avail.

The Sudan is where the notion of the all-important Coke Stop became firmly embedded in our group psyche. At home, I hardly ever drink coke, and never the full fat version. But on TDA, it was not only a guilty pleasure it was a full on necessity. The one that I remember the most was on this section of road. It was really hot and the day had been pretty dull. A steady headwind had taken most of the strength out of my legs, and the landscape was starting to move from sleek sand to scrubby brush. We were only three quarters of the way through and I really wasn't feeling it any more. Then far off in the distance, Mike and I spotted a concrete shack next to what looked like a derelict truck and petrol stop. As we were pedalling up all I could think was, "Please let there be a kiosk that sells coke, please let there be a kiosk that sells coke, please let there be a kiosk that sells coke. Coke, coke, coke, cold coke" For the next half hour my entire focus of desire was on that bottle of coke. There wasn't room for anything else in my head. As the building grew closer, my heart sank. It looked deserted, but then what joy, a fleet of bikes parked round the corner. Mike and I flung off the bikes and scampered inside to be met by 20 other riders all in different stages of coke satiation and a beaming shopkeeper. " Alice, I've already had THREE!"yelled Andre, "and they are really cold!". That first glug was like liquid heaven. We were so hot and dehydrated that the combination of pure sugar and cold fluid down the throat was unbelievably good. The first bottle went down before we even had a chance to sit in one of the plastic chairs, then with bottle number two we were able to relax and munch on some coconutty biscuits and gossip with our co-riders. In the corner, the shopkeeper rolled out his prayer mat and performed the mid-afternoon prayer.

Khartoum marked the end of the first segment of the Tour and we were all excited to see a proper city – our first since Cairo. None of us had ever been to Khartoum and I couldn't wait to explore the suqs (markets) and also see the confluence of the white and blue Niles. We also had a rest day to look forward to and an easy ride into the city. It was our first experience of convoying into somewhere. We all had to gather at the lunch stop and then set off together with our trucks in the front and rear. Remembering Cairo, the girls all found a bathroom in a petrol station before we set off for the final leg into the city. Since we were all so spread out during the ride, it was great to be in one big TDA group and also gave us the chance to mix it up a bit. I rode in with Luke, one of the racers, who would normally be hours ahead of me. Luke epitomised the best of the TDAers. He was from Australia, gorgeous looking, fit and competitive but although I might have written him off as just a pretty face, I would have been totally wrong. He was MD of a big concern back home and had a real interest and knowledge of world affairs and politics and a wicked sense of humour. Not only that, he was supportive and kind and ready to help the weaker riders. Altogether, a top bloke.

As we cycled through the suburbs, people waved and cheered. The tall, handsome Sudanese men in their dazzlingly white galabeyyas and the slender, elegant women in their coloured robes and scarves. Sudanese TV were following us that day and I had lots of fun being interviewed in Arabic. By this stage, I had lost all my inhibitions about speaking badly or making mistakes and just enjoyed the experience.

Marelie and I had booked into the Acropole Hotel, which is an old style colonial hotel right in the heart of the city. The minute we got there, a group of us all hit the downstairs cafe and ordered huge amounts of food, two sets of hamburgers, double chips and two milkshakes. With so many miles every day, we just couldn't get enough food. Then it was upstairs to lie on the white sheets and use the wifi. When you haven't had comforts for a while, they mean so much more and on this rest day, like on so many of them, part of me just wanted to spend all of my time lying down on a comfy bed and sleeping and eating rather than sightseeing. But the allure of a new city was too much to resist and we ventured out.

Khartoum is a mixture of sprawling suburbs and quite a smart modern city centre alongside a very old and traditional market winding through alleyways and selling everything and anything. In the suq, the sun in the open streets was dazzling, especially in the plastic goods area where everything was neon, but the minute you turned off down one of the side alleys, you were cast into a cool and welcome gloom. For a shopaholic like me, one of the downsides of the Tour was that as you didn't have much space in your locker, you couldn't really buy much. So I restrained myself and made do with a small dustpan and brush to get the sand out of my tent. This was to be one of the most useful things I had on the tour, and every night after I had finished, it would do the rounds as all my compadres came to borrow it.

The other thing, I had really wanted to see was the confluence of the Nile, where the White and Blue Niles come together but when it came to it, I was disappointed. I am not sure what I was expecting exactly but actually all it is, is a big section of brown churning water. So, don't rush over for that one.

That night, the second one on a comfy bed with white cotton sheets, I went to sleep thinking, " I am dreading getting back on the bike tomorrow." I loved rest days but the night before setting off again was like the worst Sunday night ever. You knew that you were leaving comfort and rest behind and that you were going to be on it again, and the next rest day was almost always too far away.

This was my diary entry for the first day out of Khartoum and into the Rufaa desert.

"Best and worst day of the Tour so far. Worst because there was a dreadful headwind all day and I felt like shit. But fantastic team work from Beate, Mike, Bob and me. 40 degrees of heat but I made it and a lot didn't. Best because when I finally got into camp shaky and a bit tearful, I got a pepsi and a big hug from Ruth who then put my tent up for me. Ribka went and got me soup and Ruth, Mike and Searj helped me change my tyres for the dirt road tomorrow. I have to do some seriously good deeds to pay back that karma."

As so often in biking, the next day just wasn't as bad. A highlight was having a beautiful camp by the Nile at the end of it and the chance to jump in the water. No swimsuit this time, just straight in with all my kit on and I had my new tent to enjoy. My sail tent had driven me mad for the whole first section.

In order not to repeat the performance of it blowing down in the middle of the night, I had to resort to all sorts of cunning tactics, all of which took too much energy at the end of the day. The first, was to walk for miles, gathering up every big stone in the desert in order to weight it down, another was to tie the guy ropes firmly to any edifice that was standing. Unfortunately, one night this meant tying it to what was effectively the toilet block, so I had stability but at the cost of a severe pong, and some pretty nasty noises. So, when Adrian, one of the riders who was only doing a section, a "sectional", took pity on me and offered to give me his tent for a £50 contribution to War Child, I bit his hand off. My new tent was normal. It was long and low and didn't threaten to blow away at every breath of wind. What is more, I could put it up on my own and didn't have to rely on someone else to hang on to the end of the unfeasibly long poles that came with the sail tent. This made my life much better.

By now we were off road for large sections of the route, hence the tyre change, and I discovered that I had the wrong tyres for this type of terrain. David, who had built my bike for me, had chosen perfect tyres for the road sections – my bald Kojaks - but for the off road, we had gone for Racing Ralphs because they aren't too heavy and they ride well on sand and rock. What we hadn't reckoned with was the African thorn. They were demons, about the same size and strength as your average nail but ten times as sharp. Our top female racer, Tori, got twenty punctures on one of her first days out in the dirt. I wasn't that unlucky, but the RRs were definitely not the best tyres for the job.

We were now deep into the south of the country which had just voted to separate from the north in a recent referendum, so in fact we were cycling through the world's newest nation. We met with kindness at every turn. One afternoon, I was cycling by the railway line we were following into a little town where it was obviously market day. People were driving sheep and goats in from every direction, and walking towards the town carrying big bags of vegetables for sale. The men were all smartly dressed in their long white robes and the women looked like colourful birds. I was pootling along the railway line, keeping my eyes peeled for the line of bikes which would mean a coke stop, and about fifty metres off were a group of three women, walking on the rails with large baskets on their heads. They were talking to each other in Arabic and I realised it was about me.

"What is it? " they asked each other.

"Is it a woman?"

"No, silly, it can't be. It's a man."

"Look at what it's wearing. " Hoots of laughter. "That is horrible, but it does look like a woman."

I thought I had better put them out of their misery, so I cycled up, stopped and said,

"Hello, peace be upon you. Of course I am a woman. Don't I look like one? Can't you see that I am a girl? "

Much hilarity ensued as they inspected me in my sweaty, smelly state. They thoroughly disapproved of my lycra shorts and red cycling top which they, rightfully, said were really ugly and made me look like a man. But they were fascinated about the trip and wanted to know exactly why we were doing it. When I said that I was doing it because I wanted to see Africa and because it was a challenge and that it was fun, they got it, but they also asked exactly the right question.

"But don't your legs hurt?"

That evening in camp, we were treated to two examples of Sudanese generosity. As we were gathering for the rider meeting, two trucks turned up carrying a delegation of dignitaries coming to welcome us. The local Commissioner gave a short speech, saying he was proud to have us in his new country and that he thought what we were doing was amazing. He also said that he was particularly happy to see women taking part and that he hoped that one day he would see Sudanese women doing the same thing. It felt great to be given that kind of praise and encouragement. He had also bought two big cold boxes filled with icy juice and sodas for us because he said, "I can see that you are hot and tired and thirsty. You are our guests, you are welcome. You have ridden many miles in our country."

Later on, after supper, our cook, James came up and asked me to talk to a local man who had arrived carrying a huge flask of sweet Arabic tea and a tray of biscuits. I went up and shook hands and we exchanged the usual greetings and then he offered me a cup of tea and a biscuit and we sat down for a little chat. He was from the local village, obviously poor, and said it was the first time he had ever seen so many foreigners and that we were honoured guests in his country. I thanked him and asked him if we could pay him for the tea.

"No, no, no, "he said. " It is my gift to you, I do this for you with great pleasure and I hope you will be happy and peaceful here. Blessings be upon you." That evening he came back from his village five times with a fresh flask and a fresh tray of biscuits to give us. These were the experiences that sustained us over the hard roads and hot, hot days.

And I needed that sustenance the next day. This was one of the "break you" days. The stage was only 95kms long but it was all on the dirt. The dirt roads we were following were the worst kind. They were a mixture of sand drifts and corrugations. This meant that it was impossible to get any momentum and that you had to pedal every stroke. It also meant that you couldn't shield each other from the wind as the road was too unpredictable. The temperature had risen unbearably. I was setting off as early as I could to take advantage of the relative morning cool but by 11.00 am when we stopped for lunch, the thermometer was showing 51 degrees. It was like cycling into a wall. I kept thinking to myself that the heat was too much, that I couldn't cope, but I knew I had to bear it because I still had half the distance to go. Every breath burnt and I found it hard to get enough oxygen into my lungs. There was no shade after lunch and no respite. I was cycling with Mike, Marelie and Daniel and when I looked at Mike's speedometer, we were often making just 5kms per hour on the flat. On one stretch at around noon, we hit a big section of sand and Marelie started crying. It felt like it was just too much and that there was no way we could do it, but we still kept going. There was nowhere to escape to, either physically or mentally. My only thought was, "I can't do this. I can't do this." It became like a chant with every pedal stroke. My legs were swollen and throbbing and I couldn't breathe. My skin was burning and every sip of water I took went straight out on sweat and then evaporated. An hour later, and I was lagging about ten metres behind. We had come round a bend, past a leafless, dried up tree and I hit an unexpected patch of sand and came skidding off the bike on to my side. I hit the ground with a big thud and felt my skin rip and tear. Daniel, Mike and Marelie all dumped their bikes and ran back to pick me up. I was bleeding down my arm and also across my knee and down the front of my leg. Daniel sacrificed some of his water to flush out the worst of the sand and told me, "Don't worry, you are fine, I do this for my daughters." The adrenaline had started to wear off and I hurt but there was no choice, back on the bike. Stupidly, I got back on, clipped in and set off. Ten metres later, I hit another patch of sand. I didn't have enough strength in my legs to get through it and I wasn't quick enough to unclip so down I went again. More ripping and tearing and my open cuts filled up with another layer of sand and grit. It hurt a lot and I felt close to despair. But my team mates picked me up and Mike stayed right beside me and we finally rolled into camp at 5pm, twelve hours after we had started. The sheer relief. But there were all the little evening tasks still to do, put up the tent, try and wash out the cuts, make sure you eat and drink enough, blow up the permarest (airbed), sort out your kit for the next day, try and get enough sleep so you can cope.

The next day came and it was even harder. We were on corrugated roads all day and the temperatures were the same. Yesterday's hardship had taken it out of me. I knew what I was going to face that day and I was really struggling with it. I was also tired and sore. My cuts and bruises hurt, especially the ones on my knees which pulled with every pedal stroke. But it was really the psychological aspect that was the hardest. "I can't do it. This is a nightmare. I've got a whole day ahead of me." That morning we started off through a mining area which had a few tiny hamlets dotted across it to serve the men working down the mines. The earth was a dark red and there were little hills and valleys.

Every evening, we would be talked through the next day's route at the rider meeting. Then either the night before or early in the morning, before we were up, the TDA crew would go out and tie strips of orange plastic ribbon at intervals to let us know we were on the right track and to mark out intersections. I had relied a lot on other people as well as I always rode out with Mike, but this day I was on my own as he wasn't feeling well and was on the truck. Inevitably, I got lost and found myself circling a kraal (cattle enclosure) frantically looking out into the distance for other riders or some orange tape. Fortunately, there were enough locals around to keep pointing me in the right direction and I managed to get back on track after a 10 km detour. The worry about getting lost actually relieved the negative thoughts about the full day ahead and the red dirt was fun to bike on, so the morning sped by.

Unfortunately, though I hadn't made enough distance, so by the time I got to the lunch truck I was the last person out and it was me and the Sweep for the afternoon. The Sweep was the crew member whose job it was that day to be at the very back of the group and make sure that the last people got in safely. On this day it was Matthias, a bit of a favourite with the ladies. He looked like a Swiss Lawrence of Arabia and was to be seen on occasion sitting on top of a dune looking out to the horizon with an Arabic scarf wrapped round his head. Poor man, I felt for him. That day was the slowest I have ever cycled. After lunch, the rest of the day was through fields of ripened grain. The roads were still rutted and sandy and after my falls of yesterday, I didn't clip in because I didn't want to risk taking my skin off again. Because I was on my own, I slowed down. I also had to take dozens of breaks. I found I was riding for 10 mins or one kilometre and then stopping. Matthias kept a discreet distance which I was really grateful for. I don't think that I could have coped with the effort of trying to talk to someone. I felt like I was battling myself, my bike, the road and the heat all the way. The landscape stretched out with golden heads of grain as far as you could see, punctuated by the occasional tree. I stopped under one of them for a break and Matthias came and sat and magicked an orange out of his bag for me. Enough to get me back on the bike and keep me going forward.

It was harvest time and we came across pairs and small groups of men with scythes bringing it in. I stopped for a break with two of them and joined them under the little shelter they had made from woven matting. They were both in their late twenties but looked in their forties, burnt by the sun and thin as rakes. They told me that every year they came out and lived in the fields in shelters, like the one we were under, for about two months while they cut the grain by hand. They had basic provisions and plenty of water. They were both married and had families back in the nearby town but didn't see them for days at a time while they were harvesting the crop. They said they liked it and that the heat didn't bother them and laughed at my expressions of disbelief. We shared some snacks and I set off again. The heat was blisteringly intense, and a little while later, we came across the lunch truck which was also the medical truck and was used to pick up riders who were in difficulty. Andre from Quebec was lying in the shade of the truck on a saline drip. He was diabetic and the day had just pushed him too hard. No-one ever wanted to give up, so people would force themselves on, even when they should have stopped.

One of the debilitating things about riding in the heat was water. The TDA crew were great at supplying us. We always filled up before we left in the morning, and then there was an unlimited supply at the lunch truck. For most of the Tour that was enough in terms of refills but when the temperatures, conditions or distance were extreme, they would arrange another refill point, so you never had to worry about running out. I could carry three litres and on these stages, I was getting through nine litres during the cycling day and still feeling deliriously dehydrated when I got to camp. That meant at least three full refill stops. I was using a camelback hydration system as I felt I needed to drink all the time. The only problem with that was that it meant that the water heated almost to boiling point in the plastic tube running into my pack in the back. Every drink was a five sip set of steps. Sip one, two and three were nearly boiling and made you feel hot and sick, sip four was luke warm and sip five was almost cool and was the one that counted. But regardless of how hot the water was, I knew I had to keep on drinking.

By now on this hideous day, I had been out for so long that the temperature had actually started to come down and I could go for more than ten minutes without resting. We were nearly home and came to a small town. The crew had brought out one of the trucks with cold, fresh water. I was the very last cyclist still out, so I got the bonus prize of a bottle of cool water poured over my head and was able to throw out the rest of my stewed camelback and fill it up with fresh.

A little group of Sudanese boys had gathered round the truck to see what was happening. One of them, he was about 13, had his bike with him. Bikes are a major source of transport and they are treated with great respect. Every one you see is decorated with flowers or coloured cloth or sequins. This one was a heavy iron frame with no brakes, painted bright green with big pink roses on the handlebars and a string of red green and white beads going down to the front mudguard. The boy, Mohammed, was really interested in my bike. I showed him the clip on pedals, the sets of gears, the disc brakes and the front fork to a series of oohs and aahs. Then I offered him a test drive and we swapped. He shot off like a greyhound, with all his mates in hot pursuit. I could barely pedal his it was so heavy and almost humiliated myself badly as I wobbled up the hill. The phrase, “All gear, no idea” came to mind.

The last few kilometres were ahead. By this time, the sun had started to go down and I knew I was going to make it, but even so that last little bit dragged out. We were camped in a shallow valley on the other side of the town and I just had the last hill to go up. I started pedalling and then my legs stopped. They had just had enough and so had I. I couldn't see the camp as it was on the other side and so, hoping that no-one would see me, I got off and started pushing. I made it to the top without being spotted and then hopped back on and coasted in. When I got in, I got a round of applause for making it, and that lifted my spirits. I was actually really proud of myself because I had got through it. I had made it, even though both my head and my body had wanted to give up, and it had felt like a long drawn out purgatory.

Only one problem, my bottom was absolutely burning and I was pretty sure I had rubbed all the skin off my nether regions and given myself saddle sores. Slamming down on the saddle in sweat soaked shorts for hours was taking its toll. I was too late for the medical session, and anyway having ridden with him all day, I wasn't sure that I wanted Matthias, who was our doctor as well as the day's sweep, inspecting my smarting arse. I felt like I had had humiliation enough for one day. So, I knobbled Ribka, who was a doctor, and asked her to have a look. It was quite a performance. First of all we had to evict Aman from their tent and give him strict instructions not to let anyone in. Then Ribka had to put on her head torch and I had to strip off my shorts and knickers. I dread to think what our silhouettes showed ... but over I bent and held apart my butt cheeks. Ribka had a good look and a little prod and then gave her diagnosis,

"You're fine. The skin hasn't broken and you don't have any sores. It is a bit red but put on some cream and you will be ok." She is a good friend! I was so relieved. Saddle sores were a real problem and I wasn't sure how I would have coped if I had got them this early as we still had eight countries to go.

And that was it. Another country down. We had just cycled across hundreds of kilometres of desert in crucifying heat. The empty, endless landscape of sand, with just tiny pockets where people could sustain life, was burned into my head. Boys looking after their family's camel herd, racing us along the route, spotless white-robed men going to market, and the dust kicked up by the herds of goats which stopped rooted in amazement when we cycled into view and then scattered, baaing in protest as we came through. The days had seemed endless when we were in them, but now they were done.

Chapter three

Ethiopia

"You can tell we are back in a Christian country – whores and beer ." That was the comment from one of the boys, as we crossed the border into Ethiopia. I still don't really understand how a manmade border can mark such a distinction in countries but every time I have crossed one I have felt the same. Ethiopia was no exception. Everything was different. After laid back Sudan, the atmosphere was suddenly quicker and sharper, with bustle and small shops lining the main street. The people were smaller and slender, with bright, keen eyes and golden skins. Everyone was an entrepreneur.

All along the route, I had been picking up bits of information about the country from Ribka and Aman. They had told me that it was different from everywhere else in the world, that Ethiopia was special. I had taken this with a pinch of salt, putting it down to a very natural bias, backed up by the fact that the country was not open to tourism and travel to the extent of most of its neighbours and so was little known to me. In the month that we spent there, I came to realise that they were telling the absolute truth. Ethiopia is different.

Before I got there, my main images of the country were all famine related, and overlaid with a large dollop of Bob Geldof. I had been one of the many who had raised money for the victims and watched Live Aid with my heart full of sadness for the thousands who couldn't eat and were just waiting to die. And now, here I was in a vibrant little town surrounded by quicksilver people.

The main thing to know about Ethiopia, though, is that it is very, very hilly. We had swapped the heat and ruts of the Sudan for endless, long climbs. It was still hot but because we got higher quite quickly, much less intensely so. We hadn't done much climbing on the tour so far, so the first day out of camp, came as a nasty shock. I had a bad stomach and wasn't feeling it at all but got myself together, and started off as usual with Mike. We had abandoned our peleton long ago in the dirt roads of the Sudan, but now I found that I couldn't even stay with Mike as we climbed at such different paces.

That first day there were no major hills but a constant up and down. The scenery started changing, getting greener and more heavily farmed and you could immediately see the poverty of the country. Even poorer, somehow, than the Sudan, where people had so little and lived in such a harsh environment. Daniel, a newly retired accountant from the US, couldn't believe it. He had never left America before, and never done much cycling before, so the tour was a challenge in many ways. He went on to cycle round the world, but on that first day in Ethiopia, he was horrified. "They're filthy," he said, as we passed a group of children, "and they don't have any clothes. I thought Egypt was bad, but this is something else entirely." And he was right. We didn't see any starvation, but there was clear malnutrition and many of the children were wearing rags. One of the many problems the country faces is dirty water. We were all to experience this at first hand, as almost everyone fell sick while we were there.

My first day, didn't start well. I got a puncture just as I was leaving camp and had to stop and change the inner tube. On the one hand, I was lucky that the puncture was in camp, as it meant I had lots of help and also access to the big pump, but it meant I was one of the last to set off, which always stressed me out. I liked to be one of the first out of camp, so that I could get some early miles in. Always in the back of my mind was the thought that I was slow and that I had to somehow keep getting ahead. In fact, I wasn't that slow any more as I had sped up a lot over the first two stages, but I couldn't shake that negativity . My late start was soon compounded by problems with my disc brakes. Dave and I had gone for a disc brake system, when he was building my bike, which meant I could stop more quickly but had the disadvantage of being a bit more complicated than the rubber road brakes. Somehow, I had bent my back disc overnight and it was catching. I had a go at fixing it myself but was worried that I would bend it the wrong way and do some damage. I decided that that would be a worse fate, than spending a day cycling uphill with my brake 50% engaged. I wasn't so sure about that decision an hour later. The hills were rolling but there were plenty of them, and pushing my legs against the brake resistance was exhausting. I kept going. I wanted to enjoy my first real day in a new country, with all the new things to look at, and the slightly cooler air, but all I could think about was how much my legs hurt pushing against the brake. I tried different strategies to distract myself:" What would I spend my lottery money on? What would I say at my Oscar acceptance speech? What was for dinner?" But it was no good, around an hour after lunch, I blew up and stopped.

The decision to stop for the day, to give up, was always a really conflicted one. I had managed to cycle all through the Sudan and cope with the worst heat and road conditions, but now my head and heart just weren't there and I couldn't do it. I just couldn't push the pedals round even one more time. I felt ashamed at my failure but I also felt overwhelming relief and happiness that the pain had stopped and that I could now enjoy the rest of my day. My legs were shaking and burning and then I got off the bike and sat down and it felt like heaven. It also meant I could stop the mental effort. I had been gritting my brain all day, clenching my mental teeth and pushing, pushing, pushing and now it was over.

The only small problem was that I was still around 20km from camp with no way to get there. The roads weren't busy, but there was the occasional vehicle, and after about half an hour, a truck emerged in the distance. I flagged it down, and they chucked my bike in the back. I had learnt the basic greetings in Amharic but that was it, so conversation was repetitive but very cheerful. A bit further down the road, at the top of the hill, I spotted a big group of riders having a coke stop. I unloaded the bike, said goodbye to my rescuers and went in to have a coffee.

Ethiopian coffee is delicious when I am drinking it back home in the Peak District, but drinking it where it is grown, in mountainous surroundings, served by women wearing brightly coloured robes, with a little piece of delicately flavoured cake on the side, is something entirely different. One of the only legacies left by Italy's brief flirtation with colonisation of the country, is coffee machines. So almost every tiny place we came across, served perfect espressos and macchiatos.

This cafe was very small, with a couple of long tables outside. A group of women were on the table next to us and we soon got talking and learnt the words for "beautiful" and "delicious" and "my name is". It was great starting to learn a new language, lots of gesturing and acting and goodwill on both sides. I also had the luxury of knowing I didn't have to get back on my bike that day, because the sweeper truck was going to come back and collect me.

When I got to camp, because I had ridden the truck, I was early enough to be at the front of the queue for the bike shop and the medical truck. This was good news as there were always long waits for both. Martin and Gabe, our two bike mechanics, had a look at my disc, shook their heads, tutted a bit and commiserated with me about the tribulations of cycling with the brake dragging on the wheel and then bent it right into shape. The wheel ran free again.

The medical truck was also our lunch truck. Every day it set off before the riders, carrying anyone who wanted to start riding from the lunch stop, and then stopped at around the half way mark and set up for lunch. It had to set off early in order to beat the speedy racers and make sure they would have something for lunch. It was a medium sized van, like a removal van, but inside it had been all specced out to Sharita's design. It was completely stainless steel so that any blood or fluids could be wiped off, with banquettes round the side, and cupboards for all the equipment. It was the kingdom of our Lawrence of Arabia lookalike, Matthias, often to be seen sitting on top of the truck at sunset staring romantically into the distance. I had to go to the medical truck for an embarrassing problem. I had terrible constipation. While everyone around me was diving into the bushes every two minutes with the runs, I could not go to the loo. I hadn't been for ten days and my stomach was all swollen up and uncomfortable. I had put off going to see Matthias as long as possible, but things had got bad.

I blame this problem with constipation firmly on my parents. We were brought up in Uganda and every year, we would drive 1000 miles to Mombasa on the Kenyan coast for our holidays. We would camp and had a big family tent. Idyllic in many ways, but there was a serpent in Paradise. We used the campsite toilets and Mum warned us that we had to look down the hole before we went, to make sure there wasn't a snake curled up there. I hope she was being serious and that snakes like the warm and moist conditions, but I have a slight suspicion that she was just winding us up. Be that as it may, I have always been very wary of hovering over an open hole. Bad news when you are in a camp where two toilet tents are put up every night and soon filled by 63 people with stomach problems.

So, there I was with Matthias of Arabia, explaining that I hadn't been to the bathroom for ten days. His reaction was pretty similar to that of Gabe and

Martin's when they looked at my disc brake. He shook his head, tutted and prodded my stomach a bit. "Take 6 of these laxatives now and 6 more tomorrow, if it doesn't clear up, there is a chance that it will become impacted and then you will have to have an enema." An enema? Those are not words you want to hear at any time, but definitely not when you are cycling across Africa and living in a tent.

The next day was a mando day, only 107 km of distance but with a hefty 2,502 metres of ascent, to take us up to the town of Gondar. Of course, in my imagination Gondar had become Gondor, the greatest realm of man in Middle Earth, thanks to an early childhood obsession with Lord of the Rings that I have never quite shaken. It was something to focus my mind on, thinking of Viggio Mortensen and Sean Bean was much more pleasant than thinking about the possibility of an enema.

I started the day nervously. My brake was fixed so I was no longer going uphill with my brakes on but I had come a cropper on the hills the day before, and today was going to be a huge amount of climbing, a real shock to the system after the flat of the Sudan. As I was downing my porridge, I tried to imagine riding my bike up Ben Nevis and then Snowdon and then doing a wee bit more, but fortunately my imagination failed me. I was soon to find out. After breakfast, I had another gruesome but fruitless session in the toilet tent and then hauled my swollen tummy onto the bike ready for a big day.

The contradiction of riding a big day is that there are lots of times when the physical effort, sore legs or back or bottom, and fatigue completely occupy your mind, and then there are the other times when you drink in everything around you and fully experience the country. My mother has told me not to use the word beautiful when I am writing but Ethiopia truly is. I felt like I had gone back to biblical times. In the early morning light, the farmland stretched out for miles and everything glowed dusty and golden. It was harvest time and the men and women were in the fields working with scythes and cutting through the different grain crops. Women were carrying water in buckets slung on wooden yokes across their shoulders, walking from the well to their houses, sometimes several kilometres. Where the fields had already been harvested and the grain gathered, the men were at work ploughing. They still use wooden hand ploughs. It could have been a painting by one of the Dutch old masters or even Constable. We were riding through this in our lycra with our garmins and iphones and technical energy bars. The contrast was so extreme it felt surreal, but the brutal fact of getting the bike up the hills acted as a great reality check.

Climbing is always hard. You feel that you aren't making that much progress, and the hill goes on and on without regard for how your legs are feeling. For this first mountainous stage, I didn't really know how to pace myself, and I wasn't really sure how far I had gone at any point. This was because of a very foolish omission of an absolutely vital piece of kit. I didn't bring a Garmin with me. I do not know why I made that particularly stupid decision. I think it was because I had never really mastered how to use it back home, and I also had this romantic idea that I didn't want to be a slave to it and wanted to enjoy my time on the bike rather than constantly checking how fast I was going and how far I had to go. Total and utter madness on reflection. All it meant was that if I was riding with someone, I drove them crazy by asking how far we had gone every two minutes. Mike, my cycling buddy, fortunately had the patience of a saint. If I was on my own, I had to try and guess based on speed and time, but in the mountains that didn't work very well. It also meant that it was hard for me to follow the instructions for the day's route, which told you where to turn off according to which kilometre you were at.

On this first mando day in Ethiopia, I truly had no idea how far I had come or still had to go. The mountainous terrain meant that the group were widely spread out. I passed and was passed by different riders throughout the day, so could check in, but after lunch, there was a long spell where it was just me and the bike and the hills. As we climbed up out of the farmland and gained altitude, the air started to get cooler and cooler. I was still scarred by the horror of the sun in the Sudan and so every drop in temperature was a blessing. I kept thinking to myself, "Your legs hurt, but there are no ruts in the road and the air is fresh. I would much rather be climbing than be slamming across those rutted roads."

Mid-afternoon and the after lunch slump had really set in. My "wow it is so fantastic and scenic and cool" attitude was losing the battle with sore legs, when suddenly I crested a summit and there were two of our French Canadian riders having a rest and taking some photos, Pierre and Jean. "It's only 23 km to go!" That sounded so good. Two more hours tops and I would be at our two day rest stop in a hotel in Gondar. Two days of rest and a hotel.

Heaven. From then on, I could have been on a stationary bike in a gym for all the notice I took of my surroundings, the focus was on finishing. As I rode into the town of Gondar, the lunch truck came whizzing past with Ruth hanging out the window shouting, "Go, go, go. Go, Alice, go, just a few km left!" Anyone who does any kind of sport knows that those words of encouragement are better than any energy drink ever created. No matter how tired you are, your spirits lift and you are ready to put in the extra bit of effort to get to the end. Lucky really, as the last couple of kilometres to the hotel was straight up. Agh, but what a feeling when I made it right to the top, cycled in and had notched up the most climbing I had ever done in one day – the equivalent of Ben Nevis plus Snowdon plus a bit for luck.

The joy of a bed with sheets and a fluffy pillow, knowing you won't have to leave it for two whole nights. The enormous pleasure of not having to put your tent up, being able to have a shower and most importantly, a toilet with a seat and toilet paper that is not being used by 62 other people with stomach disorders. By now my stomach was a big, swollen gourd and the laxatives had still had no effect, the enema was looming. I am not sure which thought was worse, having an enema, or having it administered by Matthias of Arabia.

That night I went out for my first proper Ethiopian dinner with a group including Aman, Ribka and Elvis our Tanzanian TdA crew member, who later went on to cycle from Kilimanjaro to Chile to raise money to sponsor Tanzanian students to study environmental issues at university. Aman and Ribka had constantly told us that everything in Ethiopia was different and in terms of food this was absolutely true. Their bread, njeera which is a bit like a pancake, is made from a grain, teff, that is grown only in Ethiopia. It has a slightly bitter taste and soft spongy consistency. You use it as a scoop for lots of different, smaller dishes, always using only your right hand. These include lentils and vegetables and different meat stews called tibs. The dishes are all labelled fasting and non-fasting which is due to the strictures of the Orthodox Church. Ethiopia is home to one of the oldest Christian churches in the world dating back to between 42 and 52 AD when a member of the royal court of Ethiopia was baptised by Philip the Evangelist. This is documented in Acts8:26-27. A central part of the faith is to keep strictly to the fasting days, which number 250 days a year, so it is a real commitment. On these days, which include every Wednesday and Friday, Orthodox Ethiopians have to observe a strictly vegan diet – no meat or animal products – and also no sex.

Aman and Ribka ordered for us and we got to taste lots of different varieties of tibs and also wat, which is a dish based on cooking onions in a dry pan first and then adding oil later. There were lots of different, subtle flavours in the cooking, I loved the spicy tibs with the spongy, bitter njeera. The one thing we tried that didn't go down so well was kitfo which was basically raw mince in chilli. It was one of those things that you think, "well I'll give it a go, it is a delicacy so I am sure I will like it," and then realise half way through your first bite that you really don't. Because all the dishes were for sharing, using the njeera to dip into the various dishes, we all sat round a circular table on low couches. As always, we ate like a swarm of locusts, starving after hours in the saddle and secure in the knowledge that we would burn it all off again. To finish off the meal, we had traditional Ethiopian coffee. Coffee is a really big part of the Ethiopian culture, economy and history. It is believed to have originated in the country and the coffee making holds a similar prestige to the tea ceremony in many oriental countries. At the end of our large feast, we settled back to enjoy the ritual. We had a lovely, elegant young woman to prepare ours for us. She roasted the coffee beans in front of us and then wafted the smoke of the beans under our noses so that we could smell it properly. She ground them with a traditional grinder, put the ground coffee into a clay pot with boiling water and finally served it in tiny cups with plenty of sugar. It took a long time but the coffee is scented and fresh and the whole ceremony made the meal feel special.

I was hoping that my first experience with Ethiopian cuisine and some strong coffee would do the trick with my stomach but no such luck. The next day, as we explored the little alleyways and markets of Gondar, I was like a bloated puffer fish, with thoughts of the enema never far away. Gondar is a biggish town and a regional centre, with a fortress in the middle. The view from the hotel over the town and to the plains and mountains beyond was truly spectacular. The town itself was busy and lively and a typical regional centre with food coming in from all around and lots of bustle in the shops and stalls. It was great just to mooch around and to know that we had another day to do all the jobs that a rest day demanded like cleaning the bike, trying in vain to dehair my legs with wax strips and catching up on emails and blogs.

That night, I woke up with a start. At last! The toilet was calling, the enema was not going to be needed. I dashed into the loo and 13 days worth of waste made its exit. Poor Marelie, my roommate had to suffer some pretty bad noises and I don't want to remember the smell. I sat there, thanking the Lord that I was finally getting rid of all the shit (literally) in my body and offering up a prayer for sparing me much humiliation at the hands of Matthias of Arabia. Finished at last, I got up ready to flush, looked down and almost fainted: the bowl was full of bright red blood. I didn't know what to do, it was two in the morning and I didn't feel like I was dying and I certainly didn't want to start waking people up telling them that I was bleeding profusely from my bottom, so I did what all sensible Brits would do, I pretended it hadn't happened and went back to bed. An hour later and two hours after that, I was up and in the loo again, same thing. By now it was starting to get light and Marelie was stirring.

"Marelie, Marelie, I think I am really sick."

Groans from the bed. "Why? What's happened?"

"I have finally gone to the loo."

"Well that is good, no?"

"No, there is blood everywhere, I don't know what to do."

"Alice," pronounced Ellis with Marelie's great South African accent, "You idiot. We had beetroot for lunch!"

Ho hum.

Valentine's Day dawned. We had been on the road for over a month, and I could really feel the difference in my body and my riding. Distances and gradients that felt impossible at the beginning were now fine. I had started to judge everything comparatively: anything under 140km and 1500m of ascent was easy. I had also re-kindled my love of tarmac. With my bald Kojak tyres on, I really rolled on the smooth surfaces and could absolutely bomb it downhill. That is the other good thing about mountainous country, where there are ups, there are also downs. Part flash and part foolish, I always raced as hard as I could downhill and usually managed to pass a good number of the riders who were much better than me on the climbs. Felt a bit like cheating, but you take your advantages where you can get them.

Back to Valentine's Day. I had got to camp nice and early to find Ruth really down in the dumps. She had been ill on and off for a while and was beginning to feel the effects of it. It's tough enough on this kind of adventure without also feeling ill and having to miss days on the road. What could we do to cheer her up when the usual bar of chocolate proffering had failed? Write anonymous Valentines to all our handsome and wonderful boys on the trip of course. I should really mention here that the TDA men were a pretty good looking bunch. One of the great pleasures of the trip was spending a large amount of time surrounded by hot, sweaty male totty, clad in tight lycra. The ratio of men to women was also very attractive – roughly five to one. So we had plenty of literary inspiration. We repaired to the relative privacy of one of the trucks, ripped the pages out of the back of my journal and got going. We were always taught at school that Rabbie Burns had created the perfect love poem with, "My Love is Like a Red Red Rose" but I feel that some of our efforts came pretty close.

"Nick, nick,
You are so quick
You make my heart go tick"

"Pretty Peter, so well named
You make us feel insane
When we see you on the bike
Ooh la la, our hearts do spike"

Giggling like maniacs, we posted our notes through everyone's lockers. A couple of people eyed us suspiciously but we got away with it. Then, we waited, with metaphorically bated breath to see the reaction, whether the boys would say anything or not and whether they would guess it was us.

As the evening wore on, people emerged from the locker trucks, with small pieces of paper in their hands, looking puzzled or pleased or both. Daniel, a young Canadian body builder, was part of Team Ruth, and we had spent quite some time, looking for what rhymed with "oil and flex", but when he came down the truck steps he didn't say anything at all and just went about his usual evening chores.

The next morning at breakfast, Daniel our retired American accountant, who was not by any means a body builder, was looking very chuffed.

"Hey Alice," he said, "You'll never guess what I got in my locker last night........."

Ethiopia was by far our most challenging riding so far, purely because there was so much climbing. It was much cooler but still hot enough that there were times when the sweat rolling down from my hair and forehead streamed into my eyes and completely blinded me. One hill in particular, I was determined to finish without resting, pushing on with the sun directly in my face, and trying to keep my eyes semi-closed so that the sweat would trickle past them. There was no point in stopping to dry your face, because five minutes later, you'd be in the same position. It was one of those things where you just had to accept that it was happening, and that it stung and was uncomfortable but that it wasn't preventing you riding and at some point it would stop.

Far more challenging than that, though, was the problem we had with the local children. Ethiopia's population is exploding. In the last three years it has gone from 83 million to 91 million, and more children are surviving infancy with the under-5 death rate cut in half this decade. Economic growth is strong and the great strides in public health have had a greatly beneficial effect. Staggeringly, over 44% of the population is aged under 14. We saw this first hand as we cycled through the country. There were hordes of kids at every point along the route. In the rural areas, they usually only go to school in either the morning or the afternoon and then only until the end of primary. Parents are usually working in the house or in the fields. This means that at any given time, there are big groups of children running around without any adult supervision.

The first time a rock hit me, I couldn't take in what had happened. I was cycling downhill and had shouted out a hello to a group of about twenty children who were at the side of the road, and then suddenly, it thwacked into my side. I was so shocked, I didn't know what to do. Then I was furiously angry. I slammed on the brakes, threw the bike round and charged towards them. It was hopeless of course, they scattered and ran screaming for the trees. I was left out of breath, fuming and with a nice bruise forming on my ribcage. That was the first of many times.

All of us on the tour, found it really difficult to accept and to cope with. For me, it was the lack of respect that it showed. Children thought it was ok to throw stones at a woman who could easily have been their mother. What did that show of the culture in the country? Aman and Ribka, suffered from it too, so it wasn't that we were foreigners, although that probably contributed. They explained that it had always happened, and that it was normalised there. Parents would hit or throw a stone at their children, so they learned how to do it, and with no adult supervision, there was no-one to stop them. They also egged each other on as they were often in gangs.

The thing that I disliked the most, though, was how it made us all feel and behave. These were children who had absolutely nothing and who were being naughty but were not guilty of a capital offence. I think all of us would have quite cheerfully whacked them, if we could have caught them. Usually after they had chucked the rocks, they would race off, and if they had shoes, they were usually flip flops or slip on sandals. Inevitably, one of the kids would lose these in his flight. Some of the riders, would grab the sandals and then put them down at the side of the road a couple of miles further on, reasoning that they would then have to explain to their parents why they didn't have their shoes. But these children had so little, and we were taking a vital possession.

Liam, was one of our quick riders. He was also a World Champion in rowing, having represented Team GB and won a gold medal. He loved Africa and was a trustee on an African health charity, so an all round good guy. But his story illustrated just how the relentless stoning, made us forget what we really were. He was riding down a hill into a little hamlet, when he was met with a barrage of small rocks. Enraged, he leapt off the bike and started chasing the little boys who had thrown them. He ran after them through the bush, into the village and then right into one of the huts. There in front of him was a bare, basic living room, with a baby lying in a basket. " What was I doing?" he asked us when he told us the story at dinner time. "I was running as hard as I could after a couple of uneducated, poverty-stricken boys, hoping I could catch them so I could do what? Beat them?" He turned back out of the hut, walked back to his bike and went on his way.

The day after Valentine's Day, we had a mini day of just 60km riding and then the prospect of a whole one and a half day's rest and a party that evening. Everyone was laughing and joking and taking it easy on the ride through the farmland. We were all giddy at the prospect of a party, our first one since we started. The theme was " Where you go" because that was the English phrase that everyone in Ethiopia knew and got shouted at us a thousand times a day.

Bahir Dar lies on the shores of Lake Tana, in the middle of which are islands, some with monasteries on them. It has a big, lively market and lots of second hand shops. It also had a great selection of juice shops. The juices in Ethiopia rivalled the coffee for deliciousness. My favourite was a duo: avocado and mango. It tasted so good and was so full of energy. Of course, it was incredibly rich and there did come the day when I had three in a row and that put me off them forever. But that was still in the future.

Marelie and I headed out to the market to see what we could buy for the party. We settled for some hats in the Ethiopian (rastafari) colours and beaded necklaces and bracelets. Even more exciting than the modest bling though, was the thought of actually putting on some make up. I had brought mascara, eyeliner and Coco Rouge Chanel lipstick with me as my luxuries. Coming downstairs with shiny, clean hair and our make up, we felt like actual women again, although Marelie bemoaned the lack of a proper bra, "Ellis, I have a mono-boob in this sports bra."

But it was our alpha female, Tori, who stole the show. Tori went on to win the women's race by a huge margin and complete EFI (every fucking inch). She actually won every stage and was a great competitor. Added to that, she had made her millions at a really young age, was fun to be around and was going to go on to study in Europe after the race. Fortunately, she was very likeable or I would have had to hate her. She waited till everyone was at the bar and then made her grand entrance. Dressed in a teeny, weeny peacock blue sequinned frock, with high heels and a big smile she said, "Where you go? With me in this dress, you are going straight to hell."

We ended the night in one of Bahir Dar's seediest nightclubs. Ribka was our dancing master. Ethiopian dancing is all about the shoulders. You have to be able to shrug and wiggle them while keeping the rest of your body, and your head, still. Think this sounds easy? Give it a try. It isn't. It is like belly dancing but using your shoulders like your hips. We were game, though, I will say that for us. At one point there were about twenty of us in a circle, giving it our all, with an audience of hysterical/horrified local Bahir Darians looking on as we twitched and jerked.

The next morning, those of us who smugly didn't have hangovers, sailed out over the lake to visit the monasteries. I was torn every single rest day between the desire to see some of the sights of where we were and the desire to just lie on my bed motionless and read a book. In this case, the monastery won, as really the only thing I knew about Christianity in Ethiopia was that it was very old and that they produced very beautiful and ornate crosses.

We landed on the island and walked up through some woods to the monastery buildings. Kids on the way tried to sell us little wooden boats. The monasteries are still active and there were monks dressed in white togas in the halls. The buildings were all very simple, but covered in the most vibrant and often violent wall paintings. Christianity has a lot of martyrs it seems and many of them were on those walls. Beautiful but fierce.

All too early on the following day, we were back on the bikes and off again. The first few kilometres went by really, really slowly. My stomach felt horrible and I had the post rest day blues. It was a mando day but I didn't make it. The last straw for me was when I was riding past a small group of boys aged around thirteen. They were obviously cattle herders because they all had cattle whips, and as I rode past, one of them used his to beat me. It was too much. I felt like rubbish anyway and the pain and humiliation of being beaten got to me and I gave up and got on the truck to finish the day. It didn't make me feel any better to give up. There were days like that. But they came and went and a couple of days later, we had one of our most memorable days of the entire trip.

The Blue Nile Gorge. On the face of it, the Blue Nile Gorge day was not going to be one of the most difficult. It was a sub 100km, a mere 97km, which immediately put us at a psychological advantage and the ascent was 1800m. That is a lot of ascending, but we had faced more, and by now I was feeling strong and hill fit. Also, at the briefing when we saw the topography sketch, there was a huge dip in the middle, so we had a major downhill to look forward to. In fact it was simple, a big drag up, a zoom down, and then the classic climb of the Blue Gorge itself which rises up from the River Nile as its name suggests. The day was glorious, like so many of our days in Ethiopia. Setting off as always, just as dawn broke, Mike and I cycled chatting away until the hills separated us. The ride began in a yellow, hazy valley, with not too much climbing. Fields of grain, interspersed with herds of fat, long-horned cattle grazing contentedly. The sun was in our faces for the first couple of hours, turning everything to gold and silver and fellow travellers to silhouettes. We passed men on ancient bicycles, people walking to work and school and small, determined groups of donkeys being herded by children or their mothers. They all had big, empty plastic canisters and bottles on their back, going towards the wells and clean water sources to collect water for the day.

I stopped for a snack break with a group of children under some trees near a stream. My Amharic had progressed enough to be able to find out their names and how old they were and if they were at school. When you had time to stop and talk to them, there was no stone throwing or violence, they were normal, curious children. I showed them my camelbak tube and they all had a slurp of water from it to much excitement, and then they looked on in respectful amazement as I chewed my way through one of my energy bars.

This one was a bright pink strawberry, one of my favourite flavours. As part of our nutrition, the TDA team gave us enough power bars for two per day. The minute we got the boxes at various stages along the route, a hot exchange trade started up as people swapped chocolate for lemon and strawberry for strawberry and chocolate. They bore no resemblance to real food and melted horribly in the heat, but they did the trick in terms of an energy boost and I got to look forward to my bites of sugary goodness. Also, the wrapping was strong, so you could stuff one up the bottom of your short leg, and then just pull it out for a bite when you were feeling low on energy, instead of having to stop all the time. I was already a long way on from those first days in Egypt when I looked forward with a passionate intensity to my short break every hour.

The climbing started after this short idyll, but along with it came the views and the road was tarmac with a reasonable gradient. At the top of the first ascent of around 600m, a group of us took time out to stop and take photos. Rolling peaks of mauve, blue and misty grey stretched out endlessly in front of us. Down, down, down we could see the Nile snaking its way through the gorge, turned to molten lead by the brightness of the sun. From our vantage point, we could also see what awaited us; a 20km climb with a gain in height of 1200 metres. That is a very challenging gradient indeed.

Mentally, it is always a difficult place when you see what you are going to have to do and it is hard. You know that it is possible but you also know that you are going to suffer, and you are torn between resting up and delaying the inevitable and getting down to it so that you can get it over with. Before the up, though, there was a truly magnificent down. Twenty kilometres of slamming down a tarmac road as fast as I possibly could. You can't go down a road like that and not whoop and yell. You are blasting through the air, with the wind roaring in your ears. Your eyes are streaming and you are balanced on your pedals, body low to the crossbar to cause as little resistance as possible. Big sweeping corners came up one after the other. Sometimes, my courage failed me and I had to touch on the brakes, but for most of them I just pushed my opposite foot down hard on the pedal to balance my weight and leaned on out. There were a few hazards; some random big rocks, the occasional hidden rut or crack across the road and a few fully-laden tankers making their way ponderously up or down. For sheer freedom and exhilaration though, there is little that can beat cramming down a long descent at speed on a bike in perfect weather.

But all good things come to an end, and much sooner than I wanted, I was at the bottom and crossing the bridge over the river. The Nile, our constant companion, following us all the way from our beginning in Cairo, giving us some respite in the burning Sudan and curling, now, through this crack in the Ethiopian mountains.

I stopped for a few minutes to recruit my strength and get my head together ready for the climb. This segment of the road was a time trial for our speedier compatriots, but I wasn't in any shape to attempt that. I knew it was going to take me a long time, and my goal was to ride it all and not to push the bike, and of course to finish the day. The difficulty was the gradient.

I started off riding with Martin, our Kenyan bike mechanic. I am the slow, steady type so watched in some awe, as he belted off up the mountain, his legs going like pistons, ignoring the steepness of the climb and giving it one hundred per cent. I gave a mental shrug, and trogged on up after him. Two hairpin bends later, I caught up with him, having a break at the side of the road, wheezing and panting with his head down between his knees. I carried on and he whizzed past me again, only for me to overtake him at the next rest spot. It was really hot by this time, and the terrain was unforgiving with the tarmac ahead and behind and the sheer granite of the mountain face beside us. We were a few kilometres in by this stage and Martin was starting to really suffer, he was rocking his body from side to side to get extra push on to the pedals, pulling hard on his arms and showering sweat. The next time I overtook him was the last, he blew up and hitched a lift up the rest of the way, but for a while there, he was definitely King of the Gorge.

Martin had occupied my mind for the first few kilometres, but now it was just me and my mind games. The climb was really tough so my legs were hurting and I felt like I was crawling up the hillside. I knew I was going slower than a brisk walking speed because I met two cattle herders on their way up and they played catch with me, sometimes going on ahead and sometimes falling behind when I hit a gentler part. We exchanged rueful smiles and they encouraged me with our few shared words and lots of big, beaming smiles. It is so debilitating if a walker passes you when you are on a bike. I really wanted to pass them for once and all but my legs just couldn't give me enough power. Whenever they got ahead of me, my frustration levels rose and I got angry with myself but that didn't translate into extra speed, so I had to try and focus on the fact that they were being encouraging and kind and not the fact that they were storming up ahead of me.

The climb was steep the whole way, but inevitably, it would increase or decrease a little. Every decrease was a Godsend and you got a bit of seated recovery but when it kicked in harder again, there was double the effort needed. I tried not to think of the whole climb and how slow I was going but to break it into chunks. When it got really tough, I allowed myself a break every ten minutes. Partly to rest, but mainly to have a small goal to focus on. Those ten minutes often felt endless, I would keep glancing down at my watch and thinking that the minute hand had actually frozen, when of course it hadn't. Elastic time, so slow during the effort and so fast during the rests.

On some sections, I was going so slowly that I got quite worried I was going to fall off my bike, each pedal stroke was a push and I was pulling hard on the handlebars to get me up. Then up ahead I saw a flattish part and off to the right a tree with some goats clustered around it. When I had imagined TDA, I had thought of myself bicycling gently through the African countryside with lots of time to stop and sit under a tree and contemplate my navel. This was laughably far from the reality, but I saw my chance at this stage to finally go and sit under a tree and, if not contemplate my navel, at least get to stroke the baby goats and feed them bits of power bar. So, that is what I did, and it was an intensely pleasurable interlude.

And then it was the last leg. I got up to the top, and clambered off the saddle. It had taken me just under four hours to do twenty kilometres. I wasn't going to break any records but I felt a huge sense of achievement. It had been a big, tough hill and I had made it.

At supper, Nick said, "This is one of those days that you will remember when you look back in five years." He was so right. After supper, we went off to the top of the climb and looked down on the long road, snaking round, sitting in silence until the sun set. Nick was another of our TDA over-achievers. A top corporate lawyer, he spoke fluent Japanese and was based in Tokyo. He was very strong and pretty macho, "Man Up!" was his favourite expression. He was also highly intelligent and perceptive and both fun and relaxing to spend time with. He quickly grew to be a good friend and one of the people whose thoughts, company and high opinion I really valued.

Addis Ababa was our next big marker. I had been to the airport once when I was about eight and for some reason it had always stayed in my head as somewhere magical I wanted to explore. I also needed a leg wax – badly. My legs were starting to look decidedly manly, which was not what I was going for. At the rider's briefing the night before Addis, our Great Leader, Sharita , read us the riot act about staying together for the convoy into the city and making good time on the first part of the ride so we could all gather and go in together. Entering and leaving the cities was always exciting but also a little bit intimidating. Our last big city had been Khartoum in the Sudan and we had spent the last few weeks cycling through desert, fields and villages and up and down mountain passes. For the TDA team, the convoys were the thing of nightmares. Someone always managed to come off their bike or crash into another rider and the spectre of a car ploughing into a group of us can never have been far away. So Sharita, was on fine fettle, and what she said, you did. She was not a woman to be trifled with.

Arrival in the city was, as always, a stressful scrum. I was never more likely to be unreasonably irritated with my co-riders than at the beginning of a rest day when we were all fighting for hotel rooms and trying to get ourselves into groups and find taxis in a strange city. When I arrived at the Adot –Tina hotel in the Bole district, it was worth it. The bed was so soft if felt like a cloud after my thermarest and the abundance of fluffy pillows gladdened my heart.

The next day was a perfect rest day, a total contrast to what our usual daily routine had become. I got up and dressed in clothes that actually made me look like a girl, and had a huge, leisurely breakfast in the hotel. Then it was off to the spa for a leg wax and a pedicure, where I met several of the boys queuing up for massages. I managed to fully charge my phone, bought some new underwear – lacy and racy – and went to the Lime Cafe for lunch where I ate Lebanese mezze and read my way through Time and the Economist. This was a massive treat as we were starved of daily news. Time for a bit of socialising, so coffee and cake with Liam, James, Bastiaan and Mika and then off to the St Georges gallery to look at beautiful things that I couldn't afford to buy. Ethiopia has some really interesting new painters who mix between hyper and magical realism with some expressionism and abstract thrown in for good measure. I fell in love with a representation of St George fighting his dragon but it cost around £2000 and I just didn't feel I could afford it, but it is a decision I have regretted ever since. The other things that really stood out for me were the carved wooden furniture pieces and the heavy silver jewellery made out of Marie Therese silver thalers which have been melted down and recycled. These Marie Therese coins date back to the 1700s when the Empress Maria Theresa, ruled Austria, Hungary, and Bohemia.They are also found in several of the trading nations of the Arab world including Saudi Arabia, Yemen and Oman. I bought a silver cross, and left feeling that I owned a little bit of history. That done, I headed for a wander through the area where a whole lot of small boutiques are located, selling clothes and jewellery both second hand and new. This is where the hipsters of Addis Ababa hang out and was full of great looking people. After a second shower, I went out for dinner at a lovely little Mediterranean style restaurant with Peter and Kim, Jorg, Kendra and Carrie. Tablecloths, cutlery, glasses and food served on a proper plate. When you haven't had these things for a while, you really appreciate them. If this had been my Saturday in Manchester or Edinburgh, I might have done lots of the same kinds of things and also enjoyed them, but with not even a quarter of the intensity and pleasure I felt on this day, when every treat felt well earned and every luxury was fully appreciated.

A couple of days out of Addis, I had changed my tyres for mountain bike ones as we were due back on the dirt. I regretted that tyre change as the road was actually tarmac until the very end. 116km with lots of ascent, using heavy, knobbly tyres on perfectly smooth paved roads, does not make for a happy day's riding. That afternoon was hellish. Screaming kids all the way along the road, with the threat of getting stones thrown at us always there. I was riding with Carrie, as she was sick, so had slowed down to my pace. She was second woman in the race and normally left me for dust. There were lots of hills with steep gradient shifts which made escaping the kids impossible and that combined with the heat of the day tried our patience to the limit. But, as always, just as I was getting to screaming point myself, something silly happened which made us laugh and put everything right back into perspective.

Carrie and I both had dodgy stomachs that day, which meant frequent leapings off the bike and rushing into the undergrowth. We were going up a particularly long, draggy hill when I had to go. I looked around to see if anyone was in sighting distance of me. There was only a group of about six children way down at the bottom of the hill, so I got off, left my bike with Carrie and went into the bushes. When I got back, the kids had all reached us, Ethiopia, after all breeds some of the fastest runners in the world. They were beside themselves with glee at having spotted a big, white bottom and were laughing and shouting like maniacs. We cycled up the rest of that long hill to an accompaniment of "Plpp, bllppp, plllpp," as the kids ran beside us making sloppy pooing noises the whole way.

At the nightly rider's briefing, one of the team would go through the directions for the next day and give us an idea of the route and where the various landmarks where, as well as distances and height gain/loss. When you were out on the road, you followed the orange plastic ribbon tape that the team had been out and tied on trees, rocks, signs along the route. My least favourite person to give the briefings was the Communications Manager, Christiano. A nice guy, but drove me crazy by being vague about everything: distance, direction, amount of ascent, whether you were on tarmac or not. His favourite response to any question was, "More or less." I have no sense of direction, and stupidly had not brought a speedometer so I really relied on those briefings and the orange tape. Relying on the orange tape was risky as local kids would often take it down. That day we had been warned at lunch that the directions had changed from the morning near the end as the team had had to move to a slightly different camping spot. Carrie and I had made it nearly to the end of our day, just about six kilometres to go. At that stage of every day, I was desperate to get off the bike. My mind was already firmly on the next tasks: eating soup, putting up the tent, cleaning my bike and the evening routine. Also, of course, I was always tired and my legs were feeling the strain, so the thought of getting lost or going wrong and doing extra mileage was anathema. The orange tape had petered out and we were on a dirt road going nowhere. The country was flattish but we couldn't see our trucks and tents anywhere in the distance. Carrie is very easygoing so she was happy to just keep cycling but I was getting stressed so phoned in to camp to get directions. It is actually extremely difficult to send or receive directions when there are no real landmarks or changes in terrain. Turn right at the third rut and follow the track to the little hill where there are some stones and shrubs, is not that useful. Every time I stopped to call in, a crowd of kids would gather round, coming from goodness knows where as there wasn't anything out there. We were heading generally downhill which was a good thing, but the pessimistic side of me kept thinking, "If we have to double back, we are going to be cycling right back up this." The joy when we spotted a piece of orange tape and then another and finally the TdA flag snapping in the wind and marking the end of that stage.

Arba Minch sits above a lush green forest. The name means Forty Springs in Amharic and you can see the surrounding lakes from the town. The lakes are fed by the forty springs and also by the river – which is called Cock River. Well, small things do become very funny when you have a long time on a bike every day. The ride up to it was different from the country we had been in. The area is very rich in fruits and fruit trees: bananas, mangos, oranges, apples and guavas. Suddenly, there was an abundance of water. Early on, I was pootling lost in my own thoughts, when I heard the sound of singing up ahead, I put my foot down a bit and soon caught up with a group of about 20 men carrying the roof of a hut. They had just made it and were on the way to put it on someone's home. Even though they were straining to carry it, they were all singing and doing little dance steps along the way and they all had time to shout and wave as I went past.

My company that morning was Ryan, always dear to my heart for helping me put my bike together at the beginning. We were riding along chatting when a group of kids loomed up, these ones had stones and threw them. I was unlucky and got a rock in the face. It bounced off my cheekbone and left a nice little bruise the next day. It made me feel despondent that a child could do that, but we kept going and it was good to be with someone. We had crested a little incline and were coasting down into the valley when three herders aged around thirteen stopped in the road a few hundred metres ahead of us, their flock was on the side of the road and they were all carrying whips or sticks. I mentally prepared myself to get hit, but in fact, they had something else in mind entirely. All three of them were standing there, facing us, with their dicks in their hands, masturbating. We burst out laughing! It was so incongruous and ridiculous. Ryan claimed that it was down to his rugged, South African good looks.

Ryan sped off and I was left to circumnavigate the lake and ride up into town on my own. The lake was gorgeous. Water stretching out as far as you could see and a cooler breeze coming in. All the fruit trees on either side gave good shade and there were flowers in abundance. I stopped for ages trying to capture a good photograph of a blossoming jacaranda tree. It was in full bloom, crammed with vibrant purple flowers. It was just outside the university, the main centre for the region, lots of bright, young students coming in and out. Some of them stopped to stare at the strange sight I probably presented, but lots of them were just too absorbed in being eighteen and with their friends to notice me. Photography was always a good excuse to give the legs a rest too. Donkey carts plied a busy taxi trade up and down the route, always full to bursting with either people or goods. There was a very memorable coke stop en route. It was right at the side of the lake, so close you could paddle although the effort of taking my shoes off was just too much. The usual small cluster of lycra lovelies was already there when I got there, resting up under the umbrellas. Behind them were the most magnificent trees, a magnolia smothered in pink blossom and a flame tree, afire with red. I felt like I was on a beach holiday, and we were all giddy as we were riding into a rest day.

I didn't like Arba Minch from the outset. There was a long, confusing climb up into town and near the top I decided to stop and have a juice because I could feel my temper shortening and the thought of the usual rest day baggage scrum was weighing heavily. I ordered the delicious layered Ethiopian speciality; avocado, banana and mango. These juices taste like heaven. There are many reasons to visit Ethiopia, but the juice is definitely one of them. Then I had another, and then I had another. And then I felt totally sick. I had probably drunk 2000 calories and I can't begin to imagine how much sugar. Gluttony always takes its toll and that was the last time I was ever able to drink the juice and even the thought of it now makes me feel ill. My only excuse was that it had been a long few days and they tasted so good.

By the end of our stay there, I had a horrible stomach, I blame the filthy hotel and also just being a bit run down from the heavy days on the road. Leaving our rest days, I rode the sick bus. It was such a relief not to be riding with stomach cramps and no energy as I couldn't eat, but I always felt a failure when I took the bus. This time, though, I felt too rough to really care and just enjoyed talking to Mika, who had come to join her boyfriend, Baastian, for a couple of weeks and wasn't riding so rode the bus all the time, and she gave it a whole new slant.

That day, though, there was a reminder of the real hazards of what we were doing. Mike with many bikes crashed. Mike was the young American entrepreneur, I spent our very first mando day on the road with. He had had the misfortune to have his bike lost by the airline in transport. It was a really expensive, spangly one, all custom built for the trip and it made the beginning of his tour extra difficult as he had to cope with the disappointment and hassle of not having his own bike and go out and buy the best he could get in Cairo, which wasn't very good. He spent quite a bit of Ethiopia pedalling with just one pedal as the other one had packed up. He then ordered another bike from the States, and it was like a long running Soap as to whether this bike would ever arrive and if it did, what it would be like. When it did, it had all sorts of mechanical quirks and problems that then had to be sorted out. He was a really generous guy, and when it finally did arrive, gave his Egyptian bike to one of the Ethiopian girls who had cycled with us for a part of the stage. She didn't have a bike of her own and was really delighted. On every stage, we had keen, local riders joining us and in Ethiopia, we had two female riders. They were our first and even though we only shared a few common words of language, as they only spoke Amharic and mine is incredibly basic, we managed to share some laughs and sympathise with each other on the hills. Having local riders join us, was a really special part of the Tour. The sad thing was that many of them would have loved to have done the whole thing but just couldn't afford it. Another reminder of the inequality that we represented as we rode through the continent.

Back to Mike. He was a good rider and ambitious, but out of the blue, he got into a situation where he crashed and damaged a couple of ribs. Ribs are a real disaster in those conditions because there is nowhere comfortable for you to rest up and heal. You can't bike at risk of puncturing something, but the alternatives were not good. Riding in the truck was a bumpy, uncomfortable experience with no proper seats or straps to hold onto, and when you did get to camp, all you had to look forward to was a tent on lumpy ground with just a sleeping mat to rest on. For Mike, it was time for some rest and recreation, and after getting his ribs taped up by Matthias, he headed off to Zanzibar for a few days, ready to come back and meet us later in the trip. It was a reminder to the rest of us, that we had to be careful and for me, personally, that I had to rack it back a bit when I was slamming down the hills as fast as I possibly could go. If a much better rider than me could come a cropper, then I had to take it easier.

We were getting to the end of our journey in Ethiopia, a long day on the pavement and then a short border crossing finale. Ethiopia had been a completely new experience for me. It had been hard in so many ways but truly different from anywhere else I had ever been. There were so many small vignettes of both pleasure and pain there. Stopping for a macchiato with my riding mate, Mike, talking about nothing and everything and savouring every delicious mouthful, before we got back on our bikes. Ribka in tears because she had been teased and bullied all day by people along the way due to her weight, and as an Ethiopian she could understand everything that was being said. The quick, lithe, sharp beauty of the people that we met. The extraordinary sight of hundreds of men, women and children walking to work or school along the road at first light, crowds coming towards us through the mist. The biblical, golden scenery in the highlands, where farming has not changed for centuries. Clouds of dust as overladen trucks passed us on the dirt roads, and we overtook herds of cattle and sheep. The bitter taste of the local bread/pancake, njeera. Trying to master the shoulder shake that characterises Ethiopian dancing in a seedy nightclub. Dirt and poverty everywhere.

Overall though, the overwhelming thing about Ethiopia was that it felt so new and so utterly foreign to me. I felt much more accustomed to and comfortable in the Arab cultures of the north and the sub-Saharan Africanness we were about to go into. Ethiopia was just different from anywhere else I had ever been. It is right in the centre of Africa and yet, to me, felt wholly apart from the rest of the continent.

Chapter Four

Kenya

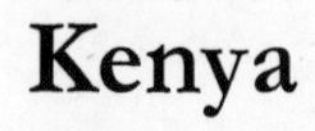

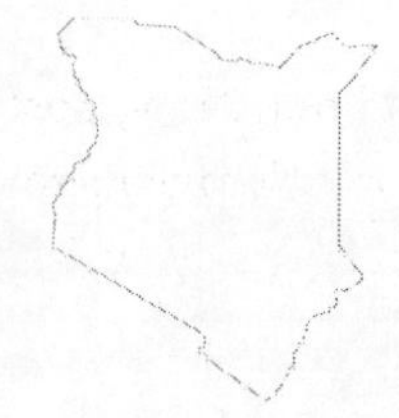

Kenya! Real Africa as I thought of it, and as was the case for many people in the group. My memories of Kenya are all from childhood and are happy ones. My parents got on a boat when I was just six weeks old and sailed off to Uganda where they were to teach for the next eight years. So, I was lucky enough to have an African childhood, running riot in the hills under the Mountains of the Moon. Every year, we would have our holidays on the coast in, or near, Mombasa in Kenya. My Mum and Dad would load up the car and drive the thousand miles to the sea along the red dirt roads.

We camped the whole way and when we got to the beach. I remember, with all the excitement of a child, being confronted with an unending expanse of white sand and blue sea. I was used to landlocked Uganda so snorkelling into a different, aquatic world was magic. I also remember the fear of trying to enter our tent when Mum had bought and tethered two giant crabs to the tent poles, ready for dinner later. That was where I gained my healthy respect for baboons, as there were a tribe of them always patrolling the campsite, and getting ready I was sure, to abduct and then eat me.

Admittedly all my road memories of Kenya revolved around being in a car going along red dirt roads through a tunnel of green on either side, keeping my eyes peeled for wild life and being rewarded with the occasional sighting of a colobus monkey. The tracks were treacherous, especially if it rained and on one memorable occasion, Dad swerved off the road and we ended up in a swamp, sinking and with no help in site. As the mud rose over our wheels a big truck rounded the corner and came to save us. Mum, had run out of cigarettes and was reduced to smoking Dad's pipe to recover.

I was also back in a country where I had a smattering of the language. I was brought up bilingually in Swahili, which is the language that was used as the lingua franca at that time in Uganda. Unfortunately, I lost almost all of it when we moved back to Scotland briefly, when I was eight. I have always wondered if it is still there, deep in some recess of my mind and could be brought back through hypnosis or some kind of regression therapy, but I have never had enough courage to try and find out. Now, post the dreadful and deadly years of Idi Amin and the equally murderous reign of Obote after him, English has been adopted as the national language, as Swahili is too closely aligned to those years.

In Kenya, though, Swahili is still spoken. My remaining words weren't that useful on a bike. Funga Malango – close the door, Toto Kdogo – small child, and Maridadi – pretty,spangly but Martin and Elvis, our Kenyan and Tanzanian TdA team members were there to help and I was soon able to count and say various appreciative things about food, the people and the countryside as well as greetings and thank you. The best thing was that the language sounded so familiar and comfortable that I felt immediately as if I could understand it or, at least, that it wasn't totally foreign to me.

Crossing the border, took the usual amount of time and waiting. We had got used to it now and had lost our European impatience at random opening and closing times, with arbitrary checking, or not, of papers. Spare time, as always, was taken up with eating and drinking. Our campsite was just across the border and everyone felt relieved to be out of Ethiopia. The constant harassment from the children and the reaction it got from us, was over at last, and we could move on to our new country and the new adventures it brought. Even though a border is an arbitrary line, the people changed completely. Now we were in East Africa, and everything was different.

A mood of celebration pervaded the camp. A mood enhanced by dinner that night. Our cooks James and Kim, were amazing. They concocted masterpieces out of very little and made something different every night. Dinner was always the highlight of the day, unless you were feeling really, really sick. That night we had a Mexican/African theme, a kind of burrito... chapattis, eggs, refried beans, mango salsa and salad. The general consensus was that it was the best meal yet. At our rider briefing though, there was bad and worrying news, James, our chef, had been taken to hospital that day, he had contracted typhoid fever. We were assured that he wasn't in any danger, but needed to be kept properly hydrated and medicated and under observation. It was bad news for anyone but there was an added concern as he had been cooking for us every day. We worried that the infection could spread. We had all had our injections, but they only act as a prophylactic and can't guarantee that you won't catch it.

Also at the briefing, we were told as always about the next day's terrain: offroad and thorny. My heart sank, my face fell. The likelihood of punctures was high and my Racing Ralph tyres were not thick enough to keep the thorns out. I was less than useless at changing my tyres and the thought of a day struggling with the mechanics as well as the road, brought my spirits right down. But to every problem there is a solution. Bastiaan and Paul came up with a cunning plan.

Bastiaan was the tallest man on the tour and towered over everyone else, his legs finished around my waist and he almost certainly weighed less than me. He was the joker of the camp, always arriving with some anecdote from the road and having made friends with everyone. He was also a great biker, pushing round the pedals with those long levers, but he stopped racing eventually to concentrate more on being in Africa. He was also very clever, and ran his own consultancy business back home in the Netherlands. He had a lot of insight into character and an ability to use that, so sometimes his questions could get very uncomfortable. I always felt on my mettle when I was with him, and really enjoyed his company.

Paul was gorgeous. He looked like a male model and the girls grew steadily more appreciative as the tour wore on and his cycling kit wore out and got more see through. Although we did regret the loss in his upper body muscle mass as Africa took its toll. He held the Guinness Book of Records, world record for cycling across America, which he did in 44 days. He then went on to smash the European one by 17 days, cutting it almost in half to 22, so he was a fantastic biker. He was also a sweetheart and would always take time to talk, no matter that I was so much further down the pecking order than him. At this stage in the race, he was lying second, after Paul Wolfe (another champion).

Bastiaan and Paul, with a gleam of fanaticism in their eyes, came bounding up to me after the meeting with their great idea. Double tyres. They reckoned that if we put two sets of my tyres, one over the other, on the rims, then I would be absolutely one hundred per cent puncture proof. The downside would be the extra weight as my bike inevitably would be much heavier. I thought about it and decided that the extra weight would be worth it, if it meant I didn't have to constantly stop and change my tyres. I remembered Tori's horrific thorn day in Sudan, when she had to mend dozens of punctures and she had the same Racing Ralphs. Greenlighted, the boys went ahead and soon gathered a crowd. There was much chin scratching and discussion about whether this was a good thing or not. There is nothing bikers like more than a bit of kit and we had been starved of it so far. So, this chance for innovation was like throwing chocolate to a dieter. The camp split in two, with some firmly against and some for. Paul and Bastiaan were in their element. A guinea pig for a new idea. When they had finally forced two tyres onto the creaking rims of the bike, it looked strange and swollen. My real worry was that the top tyre would pop off the rim and cause a horrible crash just as I was hammering down a hill. They looked totally insecure to me, but Paul and Bastiaan were soothing and convincing, or perhaps it was just Bastiaan being hypnotic. I rode the bike around camp a bit, up and down the hill and in the dirt, and it felt fine. Heavy, in fact much heavier, but fine.

I didn't sleep that well that night, thinking about what the next day might hold. I was up, breakfasted and out at first light, determined to be one of the first on the road so that I had plenty of time to complete the day if anything went wrong. As it turned out, I was absolutely the first, cycling in the very earliest glow of dawn. The bike felt heavy and cumbersome and I was very tentative with it, pushing slowly even on the descents, till I could build up my confidence.

It was suddenly "real" Africa. Red dirt roads, choking dust, blue sky and flat topped trees. I gained in confidence and just settled in to relishing every second of being just where I was. This definitely felt like home and my childhood was all around me. I was slow though, very, very slow. By this stage of the tour, we had got used to a certain hierarchy of riding and you knew where your place in the group was likely to be. Human nature being what it is and the fact that we were racing, did put you under pressure to keep that place, or better it if you could. Of course, different days and different factors intervened but still the pressure was there. So, even though I was absolutely loving the day and riding in this familiar country, right out in the wild where no tourist ever gets to go, I could feel the pressure of being slower than usual. The bike was a lot heavier, and that made a real difference. I had a serious internal struggle, when someone that I usually beat easily, cruised past me and disappeared into the distance. No punctures, though, no punctures.

The pleasure of the day was enhanced by a particularly nice camp set in a wide open plain, with hills in the distance. Sometimes, we were absolutely rammed together in the camp for security reasons or because there wasn't enough suitable ground, but this one was wide open. I pitched my tent and then went off in search of a coke. A little way up the road was a tiny shanty village, with two cafes. The one I chose, sparked off a discussion that we were to have many times on the tour, the role of foreign aid in Africa. This particular cafe, had a ceiling made up of different sacks stitched together. Each sack was from a western aid donor. They looked pretty but given the amount of them and the fact that the place we were in was still sunk in the direst poverty, you had to wonder how effective all those donations had been.

Dominating the plain, was a tall water tower with a ladder reaching right up to the top. Irresistible. I have never been frightened of heights so was willing to give it a go to get up there. Luke and I started up the ladder. It was completely exposed and quite wobbly and as we got about 30 metres up, it started to sway a little. I still felt fine, but butterflies were dashing themselves against my stomach wall and I had to try not to think too much about going up. A little further and my heart was going like the clappers, partly because of the physical exertion of climbing but mainly because I knew that if I fell off, I would die and I felt a bit as though I would fall off. Deep breathing, in out, in out and trying not to look down but just ahead. The problem was that just ahead, all I could see was empty space through the bars. Still, it was better than looking down. Finally, I made it to the top. Of course, it was worth it. The views were amazing. The flat plain stretched for miles and miles with sharp, hills dotted on the horizon. Feeling brave, I could go right to the edge and peer down at our camp and everyone bustling about, washing bikes, drinking soup, chatting, and hanging out sweaty clothes. Luke and I took pictures of each other. He had been cultivating many different facial hair styles and was sporting a Mexican bandit look, set off nicely by his straw hat. Mexican bandit and/or gay porn star. I was a sweaty mess but with an impressively heaving bosom, so we made quite a pair. The way down was worse for some reason, my legs went very soft and wobbly and I could feel the sweat spurting out of my hands, making the bars greasy and slippery. I could hear my breathing getting louder and louder, fighting across the noise of my heart hammering against my ribs. "What a stupid way this would be to die," I thought, but soon enough the drama was over and I was back on the ground, lurching as though I had been at sea and mendaciously telling the people waiting to go up, "No, it's great. Not scary at all."

How things can change in just a day. The next day was my toughest of the whole tour and the only day that actually broke me. I learnt more about myself over the next two days, than actually I wanted to know and they destroyed some of the myths I held of things that I believed I was capable of.

It was the road to Marsabit. The lava road to Marsabit. Only 86km but we had been warned that it was hard. Hearing something is hard, is one thing, facing it is another and this day forced me to face up to a lot of things. It started off fine, hard but nothing too heinous until around lunch time. Then we came off the sand and on to the rocks. Usually, coming off the sand would be a cause for celebration as you can roll more easily and quickly, but not in this case. The road ahead was composed entirely of broken, black rocks made of lava. It stretched out in a straight line with not a tree in sight. The only reason we knew it was the road as opposed to the endless expanse on either side, that looked just the same, was that it had tyre tracks along it. It was one of the few routes across this part of the country so trucks did roll up and down.

How do you describe riding on rocks? It was even worse than the ruts in the Sudan. Once again, each pedal stroke slammed me against the saddle. There was no consistency, every single one felt different and you had to push every one. No forward motion, no rhythm, no momentum. My frame was made of steel so had a little bit of flex in it and I had mountain bike forks, so I turned on the front suspension. This, coupled with my double tyres, made the bike unendurably slow and heavy but at least cushioned me a little. I could only imagine what my friends on their cyclo cross bikes were suffering.

The road stretched on, with some slopes up but mainly flat. It was a hot day, in the 40s, and the sun reflected back up off the black rock. That part of Kenya was enduring one of the worst droughts for a dozen years and as I cycled on, I came across a man at the side of the road, begging. Begging for water. What was worse was that I couldn't give him any. I only had my camelback and it was low already. I passed him by and felt, as I should, like a monster. Water, after air, the thing we really need to exist, and this poor man was sitting at the side of a track, hoping for someone to stop for him.

The lunch truck came rattling past me, full to the brim with those who had given up the fight against the rocks and got in. Their cheering lifted me for a bit, but the road soon got lonely again. To add to my troubles, the constant slamming against the saddle had brought on a bit of cystitis, so I felt like I had to pee all the time and everything was burning.

The only landmark of the day came up, a skeleton of a cow. It looked happier than I did. Every so often, I got off the bike to walk, not because it was hilly or due to any obstacles but just for a change of pain. It was getting towards three o'clock and the very last rider passed me. Sam Guo. He wasn't too far ahead and I kept him in my sights but after about 45 minutes I hit my low point, in fact my lowest of the whole tour. I had been on the bike for over nine hours with hardly any rest, my back was aching from the banging, I had cystitis, it was boiling hot, Sam was about twenty minutes ahead and I could still see him. That meant that at the very least, I had another twenty minutes to go and I could not bear it. What's more, I had done this to myself. This was my choice. That poor man sitting by the side of the road, endured much worse suffering all the time, just because of where he had been born. I started to cry, I hated my own weakness, but I gave in. I kept pedalling, but those traitor tears rolled down my cheeks. They made no difference. I still had to get there.

I did. The red flag appeared, the camp just to the side of it beside two stagnant water pools and there was my TdA family all waiting. Cheers, hugs, a precious fruit juice and a can of peaches greeted me. I was the last one in, but I had done it and joined only Tori, and Carrie to complete that day out of the women.

I was too tired to put my tent up that night, so I slept under the stars. Before dawn, I got up as usual, put my kit on and then I balked. I couldn't do it again. I couldn't get on the bike. I was fine, fit and healthy, Ribka had come to my rescue with Cypro which instantly got rid of the cystitis and my stomach was ok, but I didn't have the mental strength to do it, to get on the bike for another day on that road. I was officially broken.

I had ridden the truck before, but always with cause, and after I had tried my hardest, but this time, I was riding it as a failure. No-one else judged me or cared, but I did. I knew it was down to a lack in me, a weakness, and that I was letting myself down. It was the only day I regretted on the whole tour.

Even if I had only ridden a mile, I wish I had got back on that bike and tried, then I could have held my head high. It taught me a lesson for the future though and this Churchill quote sums it up, "never give in, never give in, never, never, never - in nothing, great or small, large or petty - never give in, except to convictions of honour and good sense."

Back on the bike with new challenges to face. We were now on the section from Marsabit to the Equator. Sharita warned us to be very careful of how we interacted with the local tribespeople here. They were known for their fierceness, and did not like foreigners, and would not tolerate their photos being taken. They were tall and handsome, mainly in tribal costume and jewellery, and almost all the men were armed with spears. The area was also affected very badly by the drought and banditry was common. I stowed my camera, and focused on the riding, not even stopping when some graceful giraffes sailed past on the side of the road. We had started to see more wildlife, little deer leaping ahead of us on the dirt roads, monkeys and these, our first giraffes.

I still had a bit to prove to myself, so this day I decided to try and keep up with the main peleton, after the first racers had sped ahead. The rule of the peloton is that you benefit from the shelter but you have to take your turn at the front. For the boys, this was a normal run, but for me, I had to give it one hundred per cent just to stay in touch and then find something extra for when I was at the front. My style went to rack and ruin and I was moving my hips like a belly dancer, but I had to dance to get enough power up. Give it up, Alice, take a break," from Luke, but I gritted my teeth and finished my turn. By the time I got to the back, and as we hit a hill, I started to lose touch. Big Bram saw what was happening, and won my eternal gratitude by coming up behind me, putting one strong hand on my back and pushing me up that slope, without dropping pace, till I caught back on to a back wheel. Seventy kilometres sped past, my best speed on the Tour so far, thanks to the lessons of the Lava road, and the generosity of the male riders, who all helped me through. The lunch truck loomed and I thanked all the Gods and determined to take it easy that afternoon. But something was wrong, the TdA team were shouting at us to hurry and bring our bikes down. "Had we seen the other riders, where were they? When was the last time we had seen the group behind us?".

There was a rumbling on the road. A convoy of armed vehicles and trucks carrying Kenyan troops rumbled past. Sharita was at the front, riding in the lead vehicle. General Sharita? What was happening? We were told that the race was abandoned for that day and we all had to ride the trucks together to camp. It would not affect anyone's standing or EFI status and there was to be no argument. Over the next few confusing hours, the story emerged.

Kendra had been riding on her own, when she heard a shout and a rock flew out of the air and hit her. She kept pedalling as the men then threw a spear over her head and fired a shot. She was badly hurt by the rock but kept her presence of mind and kept going till she got to the next village where she was safe and could get help.

There was a group of cyclists, three men and three women, a little way behind her. They couldn't see anything but heard the commotion and decided to hang back a little. Taking advantage of the stop, the girls went into the bushes for a pee break and everyone relaxed. Out of nowhere, the group was surrounded by several armed men. The men fired shots over their heads. There was furious noise and commotion. Their bags were taken from them and all the cameras, money, phones but also food and water emptied out. The men were violent and pulled down some of the women's clothing to search them. They were all made to kneel on the ground with their hands up. The riders acted with huge courage and intelligence. Instead of resisting or fighting back, they obeyed all the orders and tried to talk calmly and soothingly to the bandits. The women were hit, one getting a rifle bashed into her face, but they still didn't react. This certainly kept them safe and stopped the violence escalating. The ordeal lasted for around half an hour, with shots constantly being fired, until the men had got all they wanted and went off. The riders made it to the next village, where they were later picked up by the TdA team.

When Sharita heard what had happened, she immediately went into action. She managed to mobilise the Kenyan army, who had patrols in the area as bandit attacks were not uncommon, although usually they happened to trucks or buses. She went back down the route to collect the afflicted riders and also any others who were still all unwittingly en route. Kendra's injuries were attended to and everyone was gathered up and brought to camp. The soldiers went on to try and find the bandits but they were long gone.

Back at camp, we tried to take it all in. It was very hard for those who had been attacked. We still had a long way to go and the very nature of the adventure meant that you were out on the road on your own or in a very small group for large parts of the day. At the meeting that night, we were told the story and warned not to cycle on our own for the next few days until we reached safer country and to make sure we were cautious at all times.

It was a stark reminder that we were far from our homes and the safety and security we had got so used to, that we were in a place where people get killed often, that drought and hardship make people do desperate things and that human life is not sacred and is very fragile. It was a sober bunch that set off the next day.

A new instrument of torture. The sticky road. For no apparent reason whatsoever, Mike and I hit a 20km patch of tarmac road that felt like it was a magnet and we were the iron filings. Two long hours of drudgery. This is a phenomenon, I have come across a couple of times and never found a satisfactory reason for. I was riding in Kerry in Ireland, a couple of years before, a brilliant 112 mile one day race around the famous Ring of Kerry, and had been warned that just before the last hill, there was a "sticky patch". And there it was. No hill, smooth tarmac, but the bike just wanted to stop. I am sure there is some mysterious force, deep below the earth's crust, ready to draw us into the abyss. Our pain on this particular day was rewarded by an enormous downhill all the way after lunch. It took us just an hour to do 36km and we ended up at a hotel with a pool.

The difference between this part of Kenya and the stricken area we had just left was marked. Mechanised flower farms lined the routes. Next time you are buying supermarket flowers, check the label, I bet they come from Kenya. We'd left a region where people were begging for water, for one where sprinklers hazed vast acres of flowers for export. Mount Kenya's jagged peaks lowered in the distance and stubbornly failed to be captured by my efforts with my camera.

Back to the pool. It was quite a sight, 63 TDAers leaping and frolicking like dolphins with very dodgy tanlines in the water. It was our first taste of a more developed Africa. We were also celebrating being at the Equator, finding it hard to believe that we were there, almost half way through our journey. The thing about the Tour was that we were constantly looking forward and because every single day was filled with so many new sights, sounds, smells and experiences, we lived it fully and then forgot it and moved on.

It was good to be in cool air, on nice roads, with green on every side of us, happy, smiling people and red earth. The traffic increased, though, and as we approached Nairobi, Sharita's nerves couldn't take it, and she ordered us all onto the transport to be bussed in. Nairobi is often cited as one of the most dangerous cities in Africa, but fortunately I didn't get a chance to find out, as Ruth had Kenyan friends there, who met us and swept us up in a tide of African hospitality to stay with them at their weekend place out in the hills.

Julia and Jolyon could not have been kinder or more fun to be with. Well-briefed, they fed us with every imaginable treat until we couldn't eat any more and then they urged us to sleep in the hammocks or lounge by the pool. Being with a family was wonderful but made me feel homesick for some normality. Our lives had become so focussed and intense that it was strange to be in the reality of children having to brush their teeth before bed, and washing dishes in a sink rather than a filthy washing up bowl.

Our journey through Kenya was all too short, and just as we were getting used to the relatively easy surroundings and the gloriously cool weather - I had to wear a fleece in the morning mists - it was across the border and into Tanzania.

Chapter Five

Tanzania

Tanzania was going to be fantastic fun. Obviously, we didn't know this as we cycled across the border, but it was to end up as one of the favourite countries we went to for almost all of us. There were lots of reasons for this: friendly people, glorious and varied scenery with lots of green for tired eyes, masses of off road riding, great temperatures, but for me the main reason I loved it so much was the mud. We had hit rainy season and the roads were about to become swamps. All mountain bikers do mountain biking so they can be kids again and get filthy dirty and caked in gunge to an extent that would be unacceptable, and in fact weird, if you just went out and rolled in it. When you come back with a splattered face, talking of "awesome drop offs" and "dodgy berms" though, you get let off and if you are lucky, you might even be branded as cool.

Tanzania started off well. Just a couple of days in and we were due for our longest break of the whole Tour, three days. We were based in Arusha, the capital, and we had been looking forward to this unimaginably long break for weeks. Lots of people had arranged to meet partners there and many had booked on safaris and into nice hotels. Three days may not seem like long, but to us it was riches of relaxation and we were all determined to enjoy every single second.

Arusha is a lively, small city, with all the amenities you could want, and a bustly but chilled out atmosphere. My personal highlight was the Africafe, where they did iced chocolate Mochas. It became as regular a haunt as I could manage in three days. That first rest day, gave me a chance to experience something new. Kim had a bad throat and was suffering. It was more than a usual infection and got to the stage that he decided to go to the hospital. I went along for moral support and to see if I could help in any way. The hospital was spotlessly clean and the doctors were kind and professional. It felt very familiar, lots of waiting and then a relatively quick consultation. Fortunately, the doctor was sure there was nothing too seriously wrong, and that Kim didn't have any of the things that we all dreaded like typhoid or malaria.

The three day break was also our actual half way point of the trip and we were all reflecting on the first part of the journey. It seemed to have passed so quickly and to have been stuffed with experiences and difficulties. I felt physically like a different woman from the one that had got on the bike and set out nervously for that first ride round the Pyramids. I was stronger, fitter, browner and definitely hardier. I had been broken and had to accept lots of failures but I had also succeeded on days when I didn't think I would make it. The constant business of the day had become the norm and I had got used to a life with less stuff and more life in it. At home, I felt as if I lived much more in my head, with constant outside stimulus from radio, TV, newspapers, books, shops, friends, food, family and work. On TDA, I was forced by the very nature of the thing to live much more in my body. The only thing that really mattered was that I was well enough to get on the bike and ride it through the day. That was it. Simple. Food, sleep, the weather, hills, road conditions. These were the things that had come to matter. Yes, there was lots of stimulus in terms of different things to look at and to hear and smell and taste, but it was definitely a life of clear, easy daily goals.

How I resented, going down to the camp and cleaning and sorting out my bike on that last evening of our break. It was raining and a bit miserable and there is nothing that interesting about scrubbing your chain and getting the grit out of all the many cogs and corners.

Tanzania, the land of the hot tea by the road. The temperature in the morning and evening was so cool that a nice, hot cup of tea was just what was needed. All along the route, there were little impromptu tea shops. A square of makeshift seats made out of a tree plank balanced on crates at each corner, or actual wooden benches if it was an upmarket establishment. In the middle, was a low table or box with the milk, all important sugar and some teaspoons on it. Off to one side, the tea maker would be brewing his concoction. Thick, black, treacly tea. You really had to take it with milk and sugar, but it hit the spot. There was always a group of men, sitting on the benches having a chat and a cup or more accurately a glass, and often sporting a fine selection of bobble hats. Everyone was curious about what we were doing and where we were going and, especially near the towns, there were more English speakers, so conversation could flow a little.

We were used to being a matter of interest to the people wherever we went, but in Tanzania, this grew to a whole new level. That first day out of Arusha, I arrived at camp to something I hadn't seen before. We were camped in a wide flat area, just off the road, and near some little shops and cafes. They were doing a roaring trade, because every single person from miles around had come to have a look at the strange caravan that was TDA. There were hundreds of people standing and sitting just outside the rope that marked off our camp territory. Some were lined up along the road, which was on a slight incline to get a better view. Some families were sitting on the grass with picnics and everything we did was remarked and commented on. Martin, was a big focus of attention as he worked his way through our daily bike problems. There was general acclaim of the stand he used to hoist the bikes up on as he was fettling them. The toilet tents occasioned quite a bit of mirth and the attention made standing in line a bit of an excruciating experience, not to mention trying to make sure the flap was properly shut so that you weren't exposing yourself to the masses. It did feel extremely strange, a cross between being in a science experiment and being a film star.

This was also where I became truly aware of the changes that are being made across Africa. The programme of road building across the continent is intense, led by Chinese contractors. All through the country, we saw evidence of this, as dirt roads were being transformed. Some Tanzanians we met described it as a new type of colonisation, this time using economics and construction as the weapon of choice. On some roads, we cycled between long sheathes of plastic placed over the road surface. I am not sure why, but I assume to keep them dry or to help compact the earth beneath before laying the tarmac on top. It made for a surreal experience, as though you were cycling across a big expanse of glittery water.

Water was something which we now had plenty of. Too much of, in fact. Rainy season was well underway and we were wet for the next few weeks. Usually, it didn't rain all day, but you could pretty well guarantee that there would be at least one heavy down pour, and there was always some rain in camp. Putting the tent up became more of an art, as I couldn't let any of the inner layer touch the outer, or I would be left with a big puddle. Taking it down was a major battle against dirt and moisture, trying to keep the outer part as clean as possible, and the inner part, both clean and dry. I always lost. I also had to start bringing all my kit inside and making sure that if it was in the little porchy bit, that the tarpaulin was well positioned so that it didn't act as a big water funnel. My clothes stayed wet, except for during the hottest part of the day, when they stayed sweaty. I smelled like a mouldy cat.

The water brought with it malaria, more typhoid and some nasty ulcerations in the saddle sore department. Everyone was taking their malaria tablets and comparing the side effects versus cost ratio. Now that those clever little mosquitoes have become chloroquine resistant, our choices were more limited. I had been frightened off by the thought of hallucinations, vivid dreams and paranoia and so had decided to go for the Malarone, which was the most expensive but seemed to offer the fewest side effects. There is an enormous price differential between various tablets, but I decided this and my rabies injection, were not areas I wanted to skimp the cash on. In spite of us all taking the tablets, though, team members came down with malaria. I remembered vividly when my mother had malaria, and how ill she was, and could not believe the stoicism of those of our riders who kept going and rode through it.

Big Bram, a truly talented rider from the Netherlands, simply refused to give up and rode through it, with his bike-brother and best friend Little Bram, always at his side supporting him. Big Bram won my admiration for many reasons but one was his incredible determination. He had come into the race as one of the favourites, with a great background in bike racing, a fantastic attitude, strength and endurance. But he was to be dogged by bad luck. In our very first few days in Egypt, he was knocked over by a truck and his bike was damaged. He came out with cuts and bruises but nothing worse. However, the hours added on to his time, meant it would always be a challenge to catch up. He then got malaria but cycled through, determined by now to win his EFI, if nothing else. The problem with catching something on the trip was that it had a knock on effect, the conditions were always difficult, and there was no space or time for full recovery if you wanted to ride every inch. Bram then went on to pick up a horrible urinary tract infection, and to cap it all, an eye infection which rendered him almost blind for a time. But nothing stopped him, or got him down. He would be up and at it the next day, in the face of advice from the tour medics, who had had him on a drip the night before. Not only did he keep going, but he pushed it, trying for the win on stages which most people would have just been happy to finish. And Little Bram, always there, demonstrating the true meaning of loyalty and friendship. I found them both inspiring. It helped that they were also both gorgeous.

First real day on the dirt in Tanzania. Mud, mud, mud, rain, hills and more mud. What a day. It poured down from the minute we left camp till we arrived exhausted at the other end. Mike, my eternally cheerful and patient riding buddy, displayed a new and unexpected side to his character;

"Alice, I am riding in the truck today."

"Why, Mike? Are you feeling sick?"

"No, but I don't like rain."

"Seriously? You aren't going to ride because it is raining?"

"Yes. I don't like rain and I don't like mud. I am not going to ride till it stops raining. I am going to go in the truck."

Mike was always very definite. He knew what he wanted to do and no-one could influence him. He has true strength of character and genuinely didn't care what anyone else thinks of him or his actions. A rare thing and one which I certainly don't possess.

But I love mud, it makes everything fun, filthy fun, but fun. That day was a riot. It was a rolling hills day through agricultural land, passing through lots of little hamlets and clusters of huts. There were children everywhere, but these ones were friendly and just waved and smiled, no rocks or whips.

The roads and tracks were all on red murram dirt, which, when mixed with copious amounts of rain turn into part skating rink, part swamp and part treacle pudding. The TdA team knew that they had a big day ahead of them, trying to get the trucks through, as the heavy weight didn't go well with the road conditions. Our drivers were hugely experienced though, and knew every trick there was, to get them up the hills and safely down the other side. One particular truck I came across that day, was stuck half way up a hill, with all four wheels buried three quarters of the way up. A crowd had gathered to help and encourage, and rocks and wood were being dug in, while people pushed and pulled to try and free it. I had to go before I saw what happened but I hope it had a happy ending. The sky was an unleavened grey, with full clouds depositing their loads on us. Just before lunch, was one of the best descents ever. The road was waterlogged and slippery as ice. It had a hump in the middle, just big enough to take a tyre, with a steep slide down on either side into deep rivers of brown water. It was very fast, the gradient and the slipperiness combing to create maximum speed.

"Well, if I come off, " I reasoned, "I won't break anything, because I'll just end up in the puddles, and I am completely soaked through already."

Fingers off the brakes, bum off the saddle, body low over the cross bar, weight nice and forward to give me momentum and off I went. I went like a rocket. There was no stopping me and no surrender. That downhill went on forever, with me grinning like a maniac and holding my bike hard to the centre, adrenalin pumping, legs braced and full of the absolute freedom and pure exhilaration of a crazy descent.

The day took its toll on the bike though. I had to stop periodically to get the worst of the clay off the chain and out of the derailleur, luckily there were plenty of places to rinse it off. My gears stopped working properly about a third of the way in and by the end I had only one main cog in action. I passed several fellow TdAers in the same boat, cursing and fettling with recalcitrant machines. All our bikes were pretty sturdy, but the thick red clay was always going to win the day.

Camp that night was in the grounds of a small hotel in a tiny town and was basically a swimming pool. By the time I got in, some faster and cannier folk, had pitched their tents in the verandas or under some of the little wooden umbrellas. Bedraggled tents were tied by their guy ropes to hedges and were huddled against walls and under trees but there was no shelter from the torrents which snaked down through the grass. I headed off to find a hotel in town, there was no way I was going to attempt a tent pitch and ruin my sunny temper. Too good a day to sully with nasty tent struggles.

The next day, Mike was back in the truck, and no let up from the rain. We started off again through the farmlands and then crested a hill, just as the sky turned completely black. Heading down between two walls of stone, I could almost imagine I was in the Peak District on a rainy Sunday morning. It was cold too, we were quite high up and soaked to the skin. Down the forbidding, slope, up and over and ahead of us lay an endless plateau planted with sunflowers, with mountains just visible at the fringes. We all hopped off the bikes to get our photos taken and did our best imitations of primary school kids pretending to grow.

Martin had mechanicked my bike back to some kind of normality after the day before but the return of the mud, meant that braking and changing gear were both a challenge to be avoided if at all possible. I could actually feel the grit as the chain went round and fretted a bit about what this level of attrition was going to do over the longer term. About 20km from the end of the day we were back on tarmac again, and at the beginning of that stretch, I spotted Bastiaan, Pretty Peter and Liam all bent double over their bikes in a petrol station wielding a variety of brushes and what looked like soap. I shrieked to a halt and went to join in the car wash. The garage was supplying us with water and buckets and the brushes and detergent were cheap and communal, so it was just a matter of elbow grease. How could that much filth be on one bike? I scrubbed and prodded and scraped and soaped until I could see metal on the chain and the derailleur had re-emerged from its red brown clay cloak. The last twenty kilometres sped along easily and we arrived into a camp set on a small hill, amidst gargantuan dream-like boulders. It looked as if a giant had been playing five stones and then gone off for his supper. The sky was broiling with white clouds against a bright blue, with rainbows emerging occasionally. High spots for tents were at a premium as we knew that more rain was inevitable, and the toilet shovel was doubling up as a trench digger, as we all tried to make our little fortifications against the weather.

Earlier in the trip, the canvas strung out from the trucks had been used for us to huddle against the sun. Now, they were a bit of protection against the lashing rain, which started again the moment we settled down for supper. We were all in the same boat, squished up against each other, eating and looking out anxiously as the water destroyed our little canals and lapped up against our tent edges. My hill held out, though, and I slept warm and dry.

That was also the day that Ruth met with disaster. I was cycling in the morning with Kim and Pretty Peter up a longish hill, when Sharita's car came rushing past us. Ruth was hanging out the window,

"Alice, Alice, heeeeeeeeeeeeeeeeeeeeeeeey."

I assumed that she had just decided to give up the day for some reason and was shouting hello.

"Hey, how is it going? Where's the bike? Are you skiving?"

"I have been bitten by a dog! I am off to the hospital to get my rabies injections."

She disappeared off into the distance. What? Rabies? That evening we got the full story. Ruth had been cycling along when a dog came trotting down the side of the road in the opposite direction. Almost without warning, it turned on her and bit her on the front of her leg, breaking the skin and taking quite a big piece of flesh out. She called the team and they rushed up to get her. Matthias took her to the nearest town where there was a hospital, so that she could get her rabies injections as fast as possible. She had had hers done in the UK, but they only act as a delayer and if you get bitten, you still have to have the full course of treatment. Fortunately, it is no longer a brutal series of injections into your stomach. It made her feel very sick though and it also meant she could not ride for most of Tanzania. The wound was a biggish open hole on her leg and in the terrible, insanitary conditions, she couldn't afford an infection. It was the worst possible time to have an open wound, constant rain and damp, and endless mud and dirt. The annoying thing for Ruth was that apart from the wound itself, she felt perfectly fine, and had to miss some of the best riding of the whole trip. One unexpected benefit was that she got so bored that she took to putting people's tents up for them. What bliss to get into camp and my tent was standing there all up and ready for me to flop into. The other benefit was that she could terrify us all by showing us her tongue. A side effect of all the medication was that she got thrush on her tongue, so it was coated in a thick, white gunk.

For the next few days, we were riding through a reserve and staying at game posts. The scenery had changed to thick forestation and tall grass on either side of the road, small shambas with neat huts and blue green hills in the distance, glimpsed through the trees. The good news was that the mud had stayed the same. Plenty of it to play in. My legs were feeling good on this part of the trip. Having come through the crucible of the burning heat of the Sudan and the thigh burning highlands of Ethiopia, I was in my best shape yet. I also hadn't got to the stage where long term tiredness set in. That was to come, but not for a couple of countries.

There may have been game in them, there woods, but if there was, it was very shy and stayed well hidden. I didn't see anything, not even one little deer. In Northern Kenya, we had had giraffes and tiny, graceful buck that darted in front of us, leaping around like lunatics, and in Ethiopia we had had baboons, but in Tanzania, I saw nothing.

I did feel something though, and not to my pleasure, tsetse flies. Whenever, we left one form of torture behind, another was sure to find us. Tsetse flies look a bit like a large horsefly. They have a long proboscis with a bulb on the end of it, which they stick into you and then suck your blood through. They survive on the blood from warm blooded, vertebrate creatures – i.e. me. They are the carriers for sleeping sickness and are found right across sub-Saharan Africa. They love warm, wet conditions. Scientists have found fossils of the tsetse fly from 34 million years ago, so they are well adapted to life on our planet and unlikely to be finding themselves in the same state as the tiger any time soon. Sleeping sickness is a horrible disease as described by Wikipedia, "Sleeping sickness begins with a tsetse bite leading to an inoculation in the subcutaneous tissue. The infection moves into the lymphatic system, leading to a characteristic swelling of the lymph glands called *Winterbottom's sign.* The infection progresses into the blood stream and eventually crosses into the central nervous system and invades the brain leading to extreme lethargy and eventually to death." You can't get vaccinated for it, so each bite could infect you.

They tormented us through those days in the reserve. I would be cycling along, lost in my own thoughts and then I would feel a hard sharp puncture and a burning sensation. It was as if someone had sawn off the needle of a syringe to make it blunt and then whacked it into a random piece of my body and pulled up the stopper to take a blood sample. The stings left behind big, red, swollen welts which then itched like the devil. My theory has always been that if something itches, scratch it till it bleeds, and then it won't itch any more, but in this situation, I really tried not to as I didn't want to have open sores on my lower back and bottom while everything was so damp and hot. They loved my back and bottom, I developed a theory that it was because they were attracted to black as my shorts were black, but in reality, I think it was just the size of the target.

The red mud was still there, making it hard to steer the bike and push it through and hellish conditions for our truck drivers. It wasn't raining though, it was hot and steamy and my bike partner, Mike was back on the bike and storming ahead. A couple of days rest had turbo-charged his legs and I couldn't keep up. Every day would be punctuated by little adventures. On this one, I was pushing on manfully when up ahead I saw a crowd gathered around the middle of the road where a giant tree had fallen about twenty minutes before. I couldn't work out what had brought it down, but it was entirely blocking the road and it was big. The trunk, lying sideways on the ground, reached up to my waist. It was impossible to get round the sides because of the thickness of the scrub, so there was only one option, up and over. Fortunately, there were lots of people to help pass the bike over the top and with many thanks and lots of goodwill, I got underway again. The trucks routinely got stuck and had to be pushed and pulled and coaxed out of their muddy relaxation.

It was on this stretch of the route, that Pretty Peter and I had the brilliant idea of forming The Eating Club. Food was one of our main preoccupations on the tour and even though we were fed like kings by the TdA team, we were always looking for more. In the north of the continent, treats had been scarce; biscuits and the occasional but highly desirable can of tinned fruit. Tanzania is a poor country with a GDP of just $1813 per person which is around a third lower than the average for sub-Saharan Africa. It is mainly agricultural with maize and cassava as its two largest crops. A lot of families exist by subsistence non mechanised farming and, like all African countries, the birth rate is high. All that being said, little food luxuries were starting to become available, especially fresh fruit.

The rules and regulations of the Eating Club, of which Peter was now President and I was General Secretary, were simple. After the day's riding and either before or after dinner, everyone was welcome to come and join the group bearing a treat. All efforts were welcomed, scoffed and appreciated. A tin of peaches, a slice of fresh pineapple, nuts, crumbly biscuits.... nothing was turned away.

Every night, when we rolled into camp, we were filthy and stank like rancid buffalo. There was plenty of water around, but not always extra for washing. One evening, we were near a river. It was in flood so the water was racing down, and we could see from the bridge up above that it was the place to go to have a quick scrub. A group of us grabbed our towels and soap and clambered down the slope to join the villagers who were already there. It was like an extra-strong-jet natural Jacuzzi. I had to anchor my feet under a rock so that I wouldn't end up half way down the river, as I scrubbed away and even managed to wash my hair.

In Ethiopia, there had been a hierarchy of huts. The lowest level, was a cross between a tent and a hut made of aid sacks or canvas, but supported by wooden or clay surrounds and with its own well-swept dirt veranda. The next level up was either wooden or clay, with a thatched roof. The top level of housing was a smart, painted mud brick with a thatched or corrugated iron roof. In this rural but well-populated part of Tanzania, it was the middle level of housing that prevailed. We passed tidy little farms (shambas) comprising a clay hut or two in a compound with a packed dirt courtyard and some surrounding crops. These were usually worked by hand by the women. There would also be a few fat chickens scratching for tasty bits and sometimes a goat or two. There were children everywhere, smiling and chasing us good-naturedly.

Bastiaan, our super-tall Dutchman was a source of fascination and entertainment for them. He was a masterful communicator and physical clown, so drew crowds wherever he went. One evening when I cycled into camp, surrounded by the crowds that I had now got semi-used to, I saw a larger than normal gathering round a tree. There was Bastiaan, up at the top of it, perched precariously on a branch, flanked by highly excited boys who were loving this new form of monkey.

Mud was our primary combatant, but as we got to the end of this stretch, sand made a sneaky come back. It was fun terrain to cycle in, little hills up and down, so you could get some speed up and give it a bit of power. I channelled my boy racer and developed a technique of getting out of the saddle and pushing as hard as I could to the crest of the hill, then sitting down and getting into my highest gear at the top and really putting my weight down on the pedals to go as fast as I could. Then, when I hit the sandy valleys at the bottom, I would have enough speed to get through with strong arms on the handlebars to stop me swerving into oblivion. I was quite pleased with myself for developing this style and began to think I was quite the rider.

Inevitably, pride comes before a fall and so it was. I had got up to the top of a nice little hill, was bombing down, when I hit some unplanned sand half way. It took me by surprise and I just wasn't strong enough to keep the handlebars straight. Bang, flip, crash. I veered sharply right and walloped into the bank. My feet unclipped themselves, and I did a full somersault over the bars, landing on my back full length and looking up at a strangely revolving sky. I lay there for a few seconds, a bit dazed and confused and then looked around. There were two African men, carrying big stacks of kindling, a little way back up the hill. One was standing, frozen in horror, with his hands over his eyes. The other, put his big bundle down and started running towards me, galvanizing his partner into action.

"Madame, madame, pole pole (slowly, slowly)," they shouted, as they scrambled over the bank to pull me and the bike up. I was unscathed apart from a graze on my knee, but they tutted and exclaimed over my improvidence and inspected the bike minutely for damage. Then they dusted me down and handed me tenderly back on the road. Smiles and handshakes all round and an exchange of greetings and good will and I was off on my way again. I was a bit more cautious for the next few kilometres.

Our diet had had two welcome new additions in Tanzania; chips with ketchup and sugared chapattis. I need not expound on the delight of the hot, fatty chip, they taste good wherever you are, but I feel that the sugared chapatti is a food worth more international exposure. Visible and edible evidence of the widespread Indian influence on East Africa, the chapatti is a thick, flat pancake, deep fried and served hot with sugar on top. Unbeatable as a cycling fuel and totally delicious, especially when accompanied by thick, black, sweet tea.

The mud had been our challenge so far in Tanzania, but the next mando day reminded us of the joys and sorrows of climbing. It was (only) 110 km in distance but it was all hills and a lot of off road. We were out of the green tunnel and red swampy mud of the reserve and had reached the mountains we had been seeing in the distance for days. The big skies of Africa were with us again. Bright blue with banks of cloud. The flowering trees were also back, with bright yellow blossom vying with the red of the flame tree and the purply blue of the jacaranda. One snapshot stays in my mind as typical of this day's riding. I was hauling up an escarpment, riding with Liam who was just ahead of me, two women were walking down. Their backs were absolutely erect. One was carrying a plastic, gallon tank for water on her head, and the other a pile of laundry. They were chatting and laughing as they strolled down the hill. The water lady was wearing a bright yellow, patterned long skirt, a vivid blue shirt and a red headscarf, and the laundry lady was elegant in matching browns. It was all colour and life against the sky and earth and trees.

It was one of those days when you thought that you had reached the top of the mountain, only to find another sneaky peak waiting for you a little further on, but the views were magnificent. At our highest point, I had a big burst of homesickness. Heather! And something that looked very like gorse. We had reached the altitude for some very Scottish-like moorland and could see right down into the valley and the town of Mbeya in the distance. Hard to believe that we had been in hot, steamy jungle conditions just a day ago.

That descent into Mbeya was a memorable one. I didn't have to pedal for miles. I did have to use the brakes though. It was tarmac and hard packed mud, but both had seen better and smoother days. Giant ruts, ready to break an unsuspecting biker, rushed up at us. My legs started to ache from bracing and my hands went numb on the handlebars. It was a rich problem to have , though, I will always choose aching over burning. The moorland gave way to pine forests, smelling of radox and darkening the route ahead.

Our last day in Tanzania. Time seemed to be speeding up. My mind was empty now of everything except the day. My body had settled down and knew what was needed of it and we had left the extreme heat of Sudan and the extreme climbing of Ethiopia far behind. This final day in East Africa was one of really varied scenery. It started in a thick mist, which swallowed up riders just 10 meters ahead. We had hills and wild forests, then extensively planted fields and banana plantations. We also met lots of fellow African cyclists – cycling not for pleasure but to get from one place to another. There was no sex discrimination, both men and women on the bikes. The women as always dressed in birds of paradise colours and long skirts. It was always great to pass and chat to cyclists on the route, you always have a fellow feeling. It was also a bit unfair as we were on our bespoke new western bikes and often they were on cast iron, heavy demons of things. The bicycle is not only used for transporting people, sometimes a whole family at once, but also crops and goods. It must have been harvest time for one particularly leafy vegetable that looked a little like a cross between spinach and kale because I passed a couple of people carrying one metre high panniers full of the stuff perched on either side of their saddles. The sacks were so big that you could barely see the pedaller in between and some of the hills proved too much of a challenge for them and it was time to get off and push.

Dennis, one of our racers, slowed down and rode with me for a while that day, which was a treat. There was still plenty of climbing, a 20km straight stretch of it in fact with another 100km of undulating road, but it was on tarmac and felt easy. My rest day buddy, Nick, was also back and I kept passing by him on the road. He was much faster than me, but stopped for regular fag breaks, which gave me a chance to catch up. The three of us stopped for a hot, sociable tea, a few kilometres short of the border, to fortify ourselves for the bureaucracy ahead.

The border was chaotic and for the first time on the trip, we got mobbed by people wanting to change money. The change from the Tanzanian shilling to the Malawi Kwacha involved lots of zeros and my head was spinning. I decided that lunch was needed first, well extra lunch, and so ordered up the speciality of the house, a chip omelette. Why is this not a more popular dish? Chips and omelette with ketchup all in one, what could be more delicious? I was tucking in happily amidst a group of like-stomached TDAers when in stormed Dennis. Usually the most mild-mannered of men, he was in a rage, his face was all red and he was swearing and berating himself.

"I am so, so stupid. I am a real idiot. How could I be such a fool?"

"What happened?"

"I changed money and they cheated me completely. The guy was really very clever, he tried three things and then he got me. Sharita warned us about all those money changers last night so I was careful, but I wanted a SIM card. I stopped just outside town and this guy went and got a sim card and charged it, all for a good price, so he built trust. Then, he offered me a little more than the rate that the others were offering. I thought it was a good deal, so I agreed to change 50 dollars. And this is where he was really, really clever. Twice he counted out the bills in front of me, but he was missing one, and I thought I was so smart, pointing that out. He said, "oh sorry, sorry" and then on the third time he added the extra bill and I was satisfied and pleased that I had stopped him from cheating me. I took the money and gave him my 50 dollars and rode off. Then, I realised, he had only exchanged me a tenth of the value! He had only given me the money for five dollars."

Dennis wasn't an idiot, it was really easy to do. You get 691.32 kwacha to the pound so you can imagine the mental arithmetic involved. Added to that the confusion of changing from the shilling which was standing at 2752 shillings to one pound and it was too much. We weren't in Malawi for very long which was just as well because I never managed to get my head round how much things cost.

The last memory of Tanzania and the first of Malawi was an enormous sex education billboard right at the border. It had a man and a woman standing in their underwear facing each other. The man was standing with his arms crossed, while the woman shone a very large torch into his y-fronts. Speculation amongst the group was rife and ribald.

Chapter Six

Malawi

Poor old Malawi, I felt like it never really had a chance coming after Tanzania. We had had such a blast in the mud, the game reserves, the forests, the hills, and the rain. It was going to be a tough act to follow and we were only in the country for a few days.

That first night, though, turned out to be a memorable one. Sharita had warned us at the previous evening's rider meeting that the Rice Camp, which is where we were headed, was not a good one. She said it was low lying and muddy and that we had to be extra careful of our stuff as things were always stolen from that particular place. In fact, she had hired a couple of local guys as security guards for the night to try and minimise the risk.

When we got to the camp, it was grim. It was aptly named as it was actually a paddy field. It had been raining steadily all afternoon and it didn't let up for the evening, so everything was soggy and there was plenty of mud to trample onto your sleeping bag and mat if you weren't careful. We were once again surrounded by hundreds of people from the local village, so no privacy to pee except in the rancid toilet tent. Sharita had also made me rather paranoid about my stuff, so I had my bike right beside my tent and instead of going and socialising, I hovered near it, just in case. The other thing I had failed to bring with me, as well as the garmin, was a bike lock. Stupid.

We had had stuff stolen sporadically right along the route, but mainly if it was left outside the tents on the periphery of the camp. Some stuff wasn't important, but there was much wailing and gnashing of teeth when earlier in the Tour, an enterprising thief snatched one cyclist's cycling shoes from just inside the tent flap while he was sleeping. They were clip shoes, so clipped to the pedals to give more stability and power on the bike and were not to be found on sale again till we got to Namibia. It was a bad loss.

After a fitful night's sleeping, due partly to the spreading wet patches in my tent, and secondly to anxiety about my stuff getting nicked, I got up for breakfast, to see if we all still had our possessions intact. Good news, everything was there. But then, a thunderous-faced Sharita stalked past, yelling as she went. Two shame-faced security guards were dragged in front of her.

"Where is it? What have you done with it?"

"We don't know, Madam."

"You were meant to be guarding the camp all night. What were you doing? How could you miss it being taken?"

"We're very sorry, Madam, we don't know. We don't know where it is."

"Well, there will be no pay for you, unless it is back here in half an hour."

"Yes, Madam, thank you, Madam."

With that, they disappeared off towards the village and we all waited to see what was going to be brought back, enthralled by this bit of drama in our mundane routine.

It was........... one of the toilet tents!

A little song started doing the rounds after that with the witty refrain, "Who stole the shitter?"

That day was a bit different as we were to cycle to the nearest town to buy food for the next couple of days when we would be camping by the lake. A beach, for the first time since we left the Sinai. The Australians and South Africans sprang into action. If there was a beach, there was definitely going to be sausages, beers and a barbeque. So, we all made our way to the nearest small store and raided it. I found yogurt and biscuits and chocolate as well as sausages and bread, a veritable feast. That evening, Andre was chef and cooked up a storm and we all lay out on the sand by the water of the lake, watching the stars, which shone with extra brightness after the rain.

We had been told that the lake harboured bilharzia or schistosomiasis. If you are unlucky enough to get it, it presents initially as a kind of general malaise or flu. You just don't feel well.

If schistosomiasis is not treated, the parasites remain in your body and will go on to cause further symptoms. The immune system reacting to the eggs may damage your organs, but fails to kill the parasites. The symptoms of chronic schistosomiasis depend on where in the body the parasites have travelled to. But all the symptoms are pretty bad ranging from severe diarrhoea, to coughing up blood, seizures, paralysis in the legs and incontinence.

You get it from little worm like parasites that burrow under your skin and then crawl over your body to get as near to the abdomen as they can to lay their eggs which then feed happily off whichever organ they end up in. They are carried in dirty water, usually containing faeces or urine. Ugh. Disgusting. I definitely did not want to encounter this particular hazard so I didn't even dip my toes in. It was silly really, considering that I had swum in the Nile and immersed myself in filthy canals further up the continent, but there it had been that or die of heat exhaustion and here in Malawi it was cool and pleasant. Also, the temptation to go in the Lake was relatively slight as it was choppy at the edges, churning up brown dirt and mud from the rains. If it had been a clean and endless stretch of blue, I might have braved the worms.

Walking along the beach was great though, and we all enjoyed what felt like a real holiday. We ate and drank and read in the communal sitting room and bar or lounged out by the water. The energetic ones played volleyball – I cheered from the sidelines – and some crazy folk went off for an extra bike ride. Things were definitely easing up now we had crossed the Equator.

Unbelievably, we were now over half way through our journey and our daily routine had got settled and rhythmic. There were variations of course according to terrain, health, temperature and Acts of God, but this is what the vast majority of days looked like for me.

My alarm would go off at either 4.30 or 5.30 am depending on what time dawn was. That was about an hour before first light. I would press snooze once and have an extra ten minutes of long lie. Then it was time to grab the head torch, switch it on and exit my sleeping bag. Off with my pyjamas groaning at the thought of a new day. I was mocked by my freer American and Canadian comrades for my pyjamas but they kept me cool in the heat and warmer when it got cold and meant I could leap out of the tent for a wee or if there was a fire without having to grab something to put on, so I stand by them. First task was using the wet wipes to clean my saddle sores and then liberally apply my chamois cream. If you've never used chamois cream then reading this could change your life for the better. Chamois cream is an anti-bacterial, viscous substance that helps eliminate friction between skin and clothing, and therefore the chafing that can occur during a ride. It comes in a number of forms including balms, creams and even powder. Cyclists use chamois cream for prevention of saddle sores or, even worse, something that can leave you off the bike for several days and require medical attention: an abscess. The idea is to minimise friction and keep bacterial build-up at bay, thereby preventing any nasties. If you'd forgotten to apply and had got a bit sore after your ride, some saddle sore creams acted as a cure to help alleviate the pain, put a stop to any further problems and help prevent infection. I went through several tubes during the Tour but my favourite brand had a bit of a numbing agent in it so helped anaesthetize the pain of the first swing of the leg over the saddle every morning. It was also tingly, which was quite nice.

Then it was on with the cycling clothes, which I had carefully stored the night before. I took three cycling tops, three pairs of socks and two pairs of cycling shorts with me, so I wore everything for two to three days and then changed. Clean socks were always a red letter moment. With the shorts, sometimes I swapped them back and forth from day to day to give the pad a chance to dry out in the damp weather. There was no water for washing either bodies or clothes at most of the camps. Clothes on, I would get back to the wet wipes and wipe down my hands as hard as I could and also give my face a scrub, especially round my eyes. I wear contact lenses, daily ones, and putting them on in the tent, without a mirror and with grimy hands and face, was always a painful challenge. My eyes inevitably went bright red and started streaming, the most annoying thing was if I had put one of them in inside out and then had to go back and reverse it, with extra grime from my fingers. Amazingly, I didn't get a single eye infection.

Lenses in, it was time to start stuffing. When I had read the pre-race blurb, it had warned us to bring foam mats rather than thermarests as sleeping mats, because of the preponderance of long, sharp African thorns. I had a great affection for my thermarest though, as it had been with me for lots of adventures, and I thought I would get away with it. By the time we got to Malawi, it was covered in bits of duct tape, trying to stop up the holes, and was always flat as a pancake within half an hour of me lying on it. It still took some effort to wrestle it into its cover every morning though. Sleeping bag in its sack, down jacket which acted as my pillow in its sack, and pyjamas and toilet bag, book and diary, all got pushed back into my day bag. I had two bags with me in my locker. One was my everyday bag, which I used when I was riding, and one was my bike spares and rest day bag which I used on rest days and to store my extra bike kit. That stayed in the bottom of the locker for most of the time.

Next it was time to sort my backpack for the day's ride. I always filled my camelbak the night before and then drank a bit during the night. In the backpack, I had my two power bars, waterproof jacket, spare innertubes, pump and puncture repair kit, sunglasses, a spare pair of contacts, my camera, mobile phone, a small notebook and of course the camelback. My last job before exiting the tent was to put on my factor 50 suntan cream. I have spent far too much time outside in the sun, so have already had to have some little skin cancers removed from my face, and generally burn like a Scottish crisp.

I would throw and drag my two bags out of the tent, crawl out into the little porch and feel around for my cycling shoes and put them on. Once outside, it was time to go and grab a thick, hot, black coffee from the food table and then take down the tent. That coffee always tasted so good. Quite often the thought of it was the only motivating factor in removing me from the snugness and privacy of my canvas kingdom.

Taking my tent down was always a pain, but not nearly as much of a pain as putting it up, which I loathed with increasing intensity. Admittedly, number two tent was infinitely easier than the sail tent, but that early scarring had stayed with me. In the North, when it had been so hot and dry, we hadn't had to worry about the mud, but ever since the rains set in in Tanzania, trying to keep the inner tent clean(ish) had become quite a preoccupation.

Tent down, bag packed, the next challenge was getting them into my locker. The two big Tour trucks were home to our rider lockers. You got into them up a steep ladder, and then there were two rows of lockers on either side of a narrow aisle, each row had a bottom, middle and top locker. From day one the lockers weren't big enough, and they mysteriously shrank as the Tour wound on. There was always a queue, quieter in the morning, and chattier in the afternoon. Once I had lugged my tent and my bag up the stairs, I had to stuff them in. I was really lucky as I had a bottom locker,which meant I could kneel down and use my full body weight to push the door to, and then quickly slip the horseshoe shaped piece of steel into the lock. Sometimes I had to brace my back against the opposite side and push my stuff in with both feet.

Once this task was done, we had a bit of a breather before getting on the bikes. I would go and check my bike first to make sure it didn't have any overnight punctures. The dismay and despondency if it did would ruin the whole first part of the day. I liked to get out of camp as soon as I could, and having to sort out a puncture meant I would be late and last. Usually though, it was no problem and I would put my camelbak ready beside my bike, and go to wash my hands before breakfast. We didn't have water for washing clothes or bodies en route but the TDA team were very strict about handwashing before every meal. There were two bowls, one with soap and increasingly used water and then one to rinse in.

My favourite breakfast was good, old porridge. I would queue up to the long table where all the food was, with my expandable plate/bowl and my spoon and china mug. I had broken my spork early on so had managed to get a fork and a spoon during one of our rest days and I had my Swiss army knife as a knife. I had also decided early on that a tin mug was sore on the fingers as it got too hot so I splashed out and got a china one, which lasted the whole Tour without breaking. The table was always laid out with cereal, bread, bananas, jams, honey and sugar. Tea and coffee were a little further away on a separate table. The great thing about the buses having driven up from South Africa was that they had brought an inexhaustible supply of Rooibos tea with them. Rooibos is Red Bush tea grown in South Africa, which is naturally decaffeinated and tastes totally delicious.

Breakfast was a great meal. I always felt good because I had done my morning tasks, everything was ready, and it was a chance for some catch up and banter before the real work of the day began. It always went too quickly. As the very first light of dawn came up, Mike and I would roll, or carry if there were thorns, the bikes out of camp and get on our way.

"Morgenstund hat Gold im Mund," (the early bird catches the worm) was Mike's morning thought, as we cycled off into the reddish, golden glow. The early hours were my favourites, once the initial ouch had worn off. It was cool and quiet and we got to see the dawn rise over Africa, every, single day.

Cycling hard till lunchtime. It was usually a four to five hour stretch with a break for bathroom and maybe some photos. The toilet tents were a truly horrible option for the loo, so it was much, much better if you could, to find a nice isolated and scenic spot whilst on the road. As I got more experienced on the bike, I wanted to ride harder in the morning. It was my best time and my legs were fresh and cool. I liked cranking it up and seeing how quickly I could get to lunch. Power bars were tucked up the shorts, and I would bite off mouthfuls as I went, praying that my fillings would stay the course, those things were chewy.

The lunch truck would pass us en route and then park up around half way through the ride. When we left really early, we would be there by 11.30 but already be starving. Off the bikes, fill up my camelback, wash my hands and then over to the lunch table. Lunch was do it yourself sandwiches and fruit with whatever was available locally. La Vache Qui Rit, bread, tomatoes, bananas or oranges, canned meat. Later in the Tour, there were luxuries as the economic conditions of the countries we were travelling through improved. On one never-to-be-forgotten day, the team fried up little, juicy sausages.

If you were lucky, you got a stool to sit on to eat lunch, if not, you were on the ground. I tried not to eat too much as I knew I would not feel good on the bike afterwards if I was a pig. There was definitely a fine line between getting enough calories in and stuffing yourself. At the beginning of the trip, I would take up to an hour for lunch, but as I got stronger, I was in and out in twenty minutes maximum.

Back on the bike for the afternoon stretch, and this was when I would start to really think about a coke break. At the beginning, when there were fewer places available to have them, or there was delicious coffee or tea on offer, or I was always boiling hot and exhausted, I would stop before lunch too, but later, I tended to only stop after lunch, and usually only once. I think my record for one day was five cokes – but that was the exception.

The day was always an hour too long, even if I was loving the riding and having a great time, I wanted to see the TDA red flag and our little home of trucks and tents. When I was having a hard day, the last minutes passed like hours and the only thing going through my mind was, "Where's the flag, where's the flag, where's the flag?"

Then, oh happiness. There it was, stuck at the side of the road, usually about 100 metres from where the camp was set up. The quality of our camps varied tremendously. In some places, we didn't really have enough space, and our tents were crammed together, in others, we could virtually camp at will. In the desert areas, it had always been a nightmare trying to keep my tent pegged down, but further south, it was all about finding a dry spot, preferably on the top of a little hill, so that if there was torrential rain during the night it would pass you by. The worst ground was the rocky or slopy patch. Rocks just devastated the tent pegs, which were always jealously guarded. Slopes caused mayhem. At the end of the Blue Nile Gorge, we camped in a fragrant pine forest, and bedded down on soft, spongy pine needles, but it was on such a steep slope, that I was sure I was going to wake up in the morning in someone else's tent.

If we were in thorny country, you had to carry your bike down to the camp, to avoid the devastating morning puncture. The bikes were usually grouped in one area, and I would find a spot and gratefully, lay it down and take off my backpack. There was always activity going on, when I arrived. The racers, had got in hours before, exhausted, and were usually lying down resting or sleeping, building energy for the next day. The chairs were put out and there would be a sociable gathering of folk, sitting and chatting or reading in the shade of the canvas awnings that were pitched from the trucks. The kitchen team and volunteers would be hard at it, peeling, chopping and scraping the vegetables for the evening meal.

I was always torn when I first got in as to whether to sit down and drink my soup immediately, or whether to get it over and done with and put up my tent. Everyday, there was hot, salty soup waiting for us. It was a great way to get re-hydrated when we had been in the extreme heat, and warm us up when the rains chilled us.

Up the ladder, into the truck, pull out the little metal horseshoe from my lock and tuck it into my shorts so I wouldn't lose it, out with the day bag and the tent, then drag them out of the truck and throw them down the ladder. I do not know how my china mug survived. I had my electronics in a different bag, so they were given gentler treatment.

Searching for the perfect place to pitch was the next task. As well as the terrain issues, there were a number of things to consider:

- Proximity to the toilet tents – could be good or bad according to the state of your digestive system
- Where the loud snorers were based – some were positively operatic
- Closeness to the trucks – I liked being closeish to the trucks so that there was less distance to drag the bags. The disadvantage was that it could be noisy as that is where people congregated
- Where the perimeter tape was – we had an orange tape round the perimeter of our camp in some places, partly to act as a deterrent to people just wandering in to the camp. It was nice to be near the edge as you got more privacy, but you were also more exposed to the possibility of theft.

I developed a phobia about putting up my tent. I always, always dreaded it and hated it. I think it became the symbol of everything I didn't like or want to do on the Tour. One of the reasons I always wanted to stay in a hotel on the rest day was so that I wouldn't have to put my tent up. It was crazy really, especially when I got the second tent which was pretty easy to put up. However, that is human nature. Right until Zambia, I didn't have my own mallet, so I had to either join the queue to use someone else's or find a big stone. My tent pegs were like liquorice, so a mallet made life much easier. I also bought a set of ten fantastic new tent pegs in Zambia. They were cast iron and unbendable. Life improved after that. Once I had tent wrangled, I would go inside and arrange the interior, always in the same way... anal? Moi?

First I would sweep out any sand or mud with my little brush and pan, this would then get borrowed by all my neighbours. Then I would pull my day bag into the little foyer, and change into my camp clothes; bra and knickers, denim shorts, a grey vest (which was actually nicer than it sounds) flipflops purchased in Dongola, and a cap. The thermarest would be blown up, sleeping bag laid out and downjacket made into my pillow. Then I would arrange the other things I needed. It was actually not just a matter of being a bit obsessive. It was a necessity to know where things were when you were going to be operating with just a head torch, or in darkness. I liked to have my toilet bag and wet wipes on the right hand side in the middle. My journal and pen, book, snacks and camelbak for water at the top left with my head torch when I took it off. Clothes for the morning, I folded up and put down at the bottom of my sleeping bag on the right. I would always have a little plastic bag for rubbish beside my shoes in the little front bit, along with my bike cleaning equipment.

Every day, the TDA team opened a health clinic and a bike clinic, and long queues would form for both. Even if I didn't need to visit either, I would try and give my bike a bit of a once over at this stage, although I must admit that as the weeks wore on, it tended to be every second day. I had a very handy bike cleaning brush, a toothbrush, a rag and some lube. Obviously, in the drier areas there was no water, so vigorous brushing had to suffice. Once we were in the rains and the mud, we had plenty of water, but we had to deal with viscous clay. My bike was so good to me, though, I didn't resent cleaning it, even when I was tired, and actually I enjoyed the process of trying to poke the clinging mud out of all the nooks and crannies. At this stage, I would also pump my tyres up for the next day. We had a couple of track pumps which were tied onto the trucks, ready for use.

Once all that was done, it was time for a chill out and a talk through the adventures of the day. TDA was full of great people. Our youngest rider, James, turned 20 on the tour and Bob was in his 70s. We came from all over the world and from many different walks of life. Although a disparate bunch, we shared a love of adventure and a desire and ability to push ourselves through difficulty. Our shared experience brought us closer together. These early evenings, sitting and chatting with the TDA family were precious. The sun would be starting to go down and the crickets would be singing their hearts out. You could smell the warm earth and just sitting was a pleasure after the efforts of the day.

The gentle murmur of talk would be shattered by the words, "Rider's Meeting!" and we would all troop over for the next day's briefing. The route would be drawn or noted in green pen on the white board and one of the TDA crew would talk us through it. It was also where the day's winners were announced and the stage winners. That was always inspirational as we got a chance to congratulate our fantastic racers on their efforts. I was knackered just getting through the day, but they were putting it all out there every day, it was an impressive thing to see. For the next day, we would be briefed on what landmarks to look out for to find our way, distance, ascent or descent, road conditions and also any dangers or difficulties or points of interest. Birthdays were celebrated and washing up duties were allocated. Sometimes

Peter La Motte, an old school adventurer of great charm would recite a poem he had made up about the day. If he had had a big moustache, he would have twirled it. When we went into a new country, there would be a special country briefing, when we were given a quick history and situation report of where we were and also some useful vocabulary in the local language.

Supper was the next highlight, and it always was a highlight. The trucks had giant deep freezes in them where the team could store meat and dairy products, and they bought food all along the route. Our two chefs, James and Kim, were masters of the camp cook up. Every night was different, and I can't remember a dinner I didn't like. We always had meat, a starchy carb and at least one vegetable dish. Hands washed first and then join the queue. The hungry folk would rush to be first so they could rejoin for seconds, but I always felt I got enough first time.

After supper, it would be time for another Rooibos tea and to wash up my plate, cutlery and mug. Everyone took a turn at washing up the pots, which was a grim job, and fortunately because there were so many of us, only came round a few times during the trip. It always felt like the wrong time, though.

It was almost always dark by the end of dinner, and so I was off and ready for bed. I was usually in my tent by eight or eight thirty. I hated putting up my tent, but I absolutely loved getting into it at the end of the day. I would go to the loo, fill up my camelbak to avoid queues the next day, and get my backpack sorted, making sure to put in two new power bars. Then it was ablutions. Lenses out and as they were dailies, chucked into my rubbish bag, wet wipe scrub done and any necessary lotion rubbed into sore bits, teeth brushed and then my reassuringly expensive Lancome night cream applied. The last duty of the day was to write my diary, even more of a scrawl than usual. I have kept a diary since I was eleven on and off, so it is a real habit. Rather distressingly though, it is more of a personal record than something that would delight the nation with its wisdom and wit were it to be published.

This is a typical entry:

"Morning very hard. Afternoon had tail wind so not so bad. Legs hurt. Was very hungry at camp, then ate too much. Put tent up after dinner to the hilarity of the staff. Very dust and windy and dirty."

Writing was the last task of the day and now it was time for total relaxation, my book, a little biscuit, I know I should have had it before the tooth brushing but it was my nightly treat, and the last bit of Rooibos. Lights out with the head torch carefully placed at head level on the left hand side, and my camelbak tube in easy reach. Ten hours of rest and then up to do it all again in the morning.

It was the last day in March, and we were still in the rains. The morning weather was a bit like Scotland, so I felt right at home. Leaving the lake we set off in a soft, grey mist which soon soaked everything that had dried out at the lake. We rode past all the little fishing hamlets that surrounded the lake and looked reasonably clean and prosperous. At that time in the morning, there were still groups of fishermen getting the nets ready and starting to push their long, wooden boats out into the lake. The ride took us up over a slow climbing escarpment. At the beginning of the Tour, that long up would have killed me but after the ardours of Ethiopian mountains, it was positively enjoyable. When the road curves up relatively gently and are tarmac, in cool weather, the legs churn around quite happily. The mist meant we could only see a few metres ahead which gave everything a dreamlike quality and made you ride inside your head rather than looking about. Sometimes it parted and then there was the lake further and further beneath us all silver and glittering, its blue had been bleached out by the mix of cloud cover and sunlight.

Ruth was back on the bike and riding really strongly. Her leg had healed up and her tongue was no longer covered in a thick, white fuzz. But more disaster hit the camp that day. Three of our riders had had to go and get tested as the medical team were worried that they might have cholera. All were really strong riders – Mike, Big Bram and Paul Spencer. Paul was lying at number two in the race behind Paul Wolfe and poor old Mike with many bikes seemed to have had the worst luck of anyone on the trip. Cholera is caused by the infection of food or water by fecal matter, which is disgusting but the truth is we could easily have picked it up in any number of the camps and places we stayed in or rode through. The tests came back negative but all were positive for malaria. The rainy season mosquitoes had claimed some more victims. Malaria has symptoms like a really bad gastric flu, nausea, vomiting, fever and headaches and can cause severe dehydration. It is in the top five causes of death by disease in Africa, so it is not to be taken lightly. You treat it with a variety of drugs depending on severity and if you get it, you are meant to rest up. Our racers were so committed though that they were determined to keep going.

Once again a day changed everything. The day before, I was pumping up the escarpment with my head in a misty dream world, next day I wrote in my diary, "Rolling, sodding hills all day." It was a mando day so 124km and 2000m of climbing but without any majors, just "rolling, sodding hills all day." We ended up camping in the grounds of a school. It rained and rained and rained and then the sky cleared to give us a true African sunset of pinks and reds fading into complete blackness. I went out after dark in my pyjamas and looked at the sky with all its abundant stars showing sharply against the black, breathed in the damp smell and enjoyed my moment of being in Africa. That was the day that Paul Spencer decided he had to give up for a while and in so doing lose his EFI and his position in the race. He realised that he couldn't keep going, while suffering with malaria and not do himself some serious damage. But he stopped with total grace. Given he was in second place and was such a fantastic rider, he would have been forgiven for showing some angst or anger, but he didn't. He said his goodbyes and headed off for some R&R without a word of regret or complaint. He just wished us all luck and said he'd see us later. True character shines through when things get difficult.

The scenery had changed again. Big, wide skies filled with clouds that were either white and fluffy, or rather forbiddingly grey fading to black when the rain was coming. On either side of the road, the vegetation was lush and green and we rode past pine forests as well as banana plantations. Strange boulder shaped hills poked up and out ahead or to the side of us. They looked like they had just been dropped there at random. Little towns dotted the road at intervals. There were shops with fantastic names like: "Divine Wisdom Kasalu Shop" and "Msiyamo Coffin Workshop, Jenda Branch". There were also makeshift markets along the road with rows of buckets and plastic basins piled high with vegetables. Red skinned potatoes at the back, white skinned further forward, then tomatoes, apples and fat green beans right at the front.

The tarmac was beautiful and we were lucky that there was very little traffic in terms of cars and lorries. We had started to meet up with lots of local bicycle traffic, though. Of course, the boys and men would try and race me when I passed, clearly scandalised that this foreign woman was pushing ahead. In a fair fight, they would have beaten me hollow, but I was on a great bike and was only carrying what I needed for the day. They were usually on cast iron monsters, with lots of bits missing. Sometimes, they would have big nails instead of pedals, or bits of stick where there should be wheel spokes. We would often pass some poor soul, patching up a porcupined inner tube and pumping like crazy. I famously managed to cross Africa without really learning how to change a tyre – I can theoretically but didn't have to put it to the test, thanks to the huge kindness of my male compatriots - so I couldn't do anything useful to help my fellow bikers. Sometimes I would stop to offer them the use of my pump though, as it seemed better than the old fashioned tube version that they were using. Back to the racing problem. What would usually happen, is that I would cruise past someone on a hill, and then half a mile later, they would catch me up and triumphantly battle forwards with a huge smile, puffing and panting and legs going like an Olympic class sprinter. Then, they would immediately slow down, pride satisfied, foreign female put firmly in her place, and job done. The only problem was that that meant I inevitably passed them again without really trying and off we went again. Sometimes this would go on for miles.

There were also the taxi cyclists. I rode for a bit with an entire family on one bike making their way to a market in the local town. The husband was at the front pedalling, his wife, who was impeccably dressed in an African print wrap skirt, top and head scarf, was perched on the back, where a cushion had been put on the back rack, and their two children were sandwiched in the middle. They had somehow found room for a big, pink bag full of produce. The cargo cyclists also deserve a mention. Who knew that a fridge would fit on a bike, or enough timber to make a small hut, or a full harvest of green bananas. You often couldn't see the cyclist at all underneath his enormous load of stuff, but when you passed you always got a hello and a massive smile.

I met one man who really stuck in my mind. We cycled together for about an hour in the rain. He was going to meet his parents in a town about 40 kms away and was riding the usual big, heavy bike but kept up with me so we could chat. He was in his mid forties and was an English teacher by trade. When I asked him if he enjoyed it he said it was impossible.

"Madam, we have up to one hundred students in one class. They are all different ages and they do not always want to listen. I have to teach many things that I do not know about, not only English. The wages are very, very low so I have to also try to find other work. "

He was married, in fact he was married twice over as he had two wives and seven children. I asked him if he could manage that financially and he said it was a constant struggle but what could he do, he had to provide for the children. There we were the two of us, doing exactly the same thing, riding the next 40 kms in a slightly cold drizzle along a flat tarmac roads. Both of us had university educations and were similar ages, but there the similarity ended. I had all the freedom in the world and the means to take four months to go on an adventure, while this man had to work every hour to support his family, and still found time to cycle for two hours to go and see his parents. I hope he felt equally sorry for me, without a husband and children and without a job. I feel that would make life fairer.

As we approached Lilongwe, things started to get manicured. The grass beside the road had been cut and there were carefully planted trees and flower bushes surrounded with white painted stones. It was a jolt from the mixture of wild bush and carefully planted shambas that we had been riding through. What I didn't realise was that it was an intimation of things to come. Some put it down to the " South Africa effect". The effect of the money and expertise from that large economy filtering upwards. Whether or not that is true, I don't know. It was certainly noticeable as we got further down the continent but we were still a long way away from Jo'burg. What we could see clear evidence of, however, was that we had entered a different kind of economy.

Lilongwe is a very pretty and calm little place. We stayed in the Kiboko Town Hotel, found by Nick in his Africa guide. If you ever go to Lilongwe, stay there. It was perfect. Whitewashed walls, a lounge area covered in cushions with a log fire in the evening, and a little garden out the back. The rooms were simple but pretty and the hot water in the shower didn't run out, ever. It was right in the centre of town and my first job was to go out and find the doughnuts. There were doughnuts in a huge supermarket in the centre, where I filled up my trolley without regard to cost or locker room with a cornucopia of goodies, including salted macadamia nuts, and of course, doughnuts. I paid on my credit card, that is how sophisticated this supermarket was, and when I got back to the UK almost fainted with shock when I found out exactly how much salted macadamia nuts cost. There was also a bookshop in town and a Chinese/Asian grocery shop, so Nick was in heaven, and would whip out exotic looking treats on the next stage of the journey. That night, a group of us gathered for dinner and wolfed down enormous plates of steak and chips. I remember looking around at the group and feeling privileged to be a part of it and to be sharing time with such exceptional people.

Unfortunately, our hotel was fully booked on the last night before we set off, so I had to move to camp and put my tent up. The camp was fine, but it was pouring with rain and because I had put off moving until the last possible moment, I had to put my tent up in the mud and the pitch black. I grumbled and groaned through the whole process, definitely making it worse for myself, but then once I was in there, I had a cup of rooibos and opened the brown bag of doughnuts I had been clever (and greedy) enough to supply myself with on a second trip to the supermarket, and the evening got a whole lot better.

All too soon, and we were leaving Malawi and heading in to Zambia. Six countries down, but still four to go.

Chapter seven

Zambia

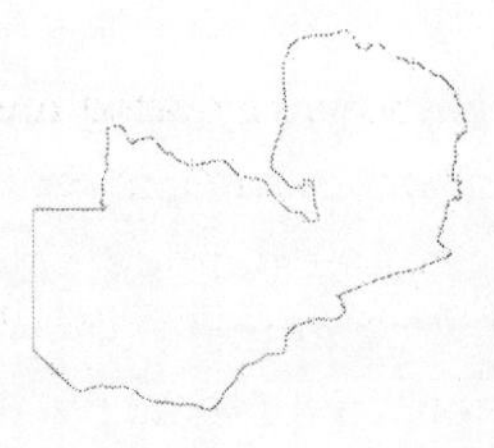

I rode through Zambia almost in a dream. This was the time when my mind really let go of everything and I would spend hours and hours on my bike, thinking about absolutely nothing, just being there. I think it was down to the stage of the journey we were at, and the length of time we had been on the road. I understood the demands of the Tour in a physical way, and my routine was set. It was still wet but conditions were improving. There was more western-style food available in stops along the way, chocolate and cakes, to keep us fuelled. Also there was a lot of tarmac and flattish stages so the terrain was very doable. I rode alone for most of the country. Mike and I would still set out together but we would soon break into our own pace.

Zambia has a very quickly growing economy although, like everything else, it is centred on the urban centres. Mining and agriculture are the two mainstays, with copper being the main mining product. In the countryside the World Bank still estimates that there are 78% of families living in poverty but in the cities, there is a growing middle class. HIV has been declining too in the last ten years. The official language is English, which made life easier if a little less interesting.

Because so many of the people were concentrated in, or around, the cities, we would cycle for long stretches and not see anyone. There were enough hills to make the line of riders stretch out and disappear ahead and behind.

The mornings were beautiful. One day, I stopped half way up a hill to try and capture the pinks and golds of the sky framed by the green of the trees in a photo. But I couldn't capture the sound of the birds, or the first flush of warmth on my skin, or the feeling of strength in my legs and absolute calm.

It was green and lush, with thick forestation lining the road in lots of areas. A combination of flat and rolling hills. In Zambia, the thought struck me more than any other time, " I am riding on my own through the African bush." The sun was warm and I was going through a green tunnel of trees, watching the tarmac, with bits of red earth poking up through the undergrowth. Little, neat clusters of huts arranged into compounds, dotted the road, all with a few chickens, a couple of toddlers and the obligatory goat or two.

Because I had left a good job, and was looking forward to a new future, I had imagined before I set off that I would spend a lot of time on the bike thinking about what was going to come. I thought that I would be both physically and mentally productive, really getting to the root of what I wanted to do next and how I would shape this phase of my life. I couldn't conceive that I would spend six hours on a bike with a blank mind. Sometimes, I would force myself to try and think forward and try to plan, but within minutes, my mind would default back to blank. It sounds incredibly tedious, but it wasn't. I felt like I was defragging my brain.

At home in the UK, my life revolves around the mental much more than the physical. Exercise and the outdoors are things I enjoy and get to do and spend time on, but the majority of my days would be in an office. We left in January, so I had just undergone the usual winter trauma of hardly ever being in natural light, and in natural temperatures. My central heating is always up to the max when I am at home, and offices are universally overheated.

On TDA, that reversed and we were all concerned much more with the physical than the mental. What really mattered was how your legs felt, what the weather was like, did you feel hot or cold, were you hungry, was it lunch yet? When was the next coke stop, what could you hear, how did the sun feel, was anything uncomfortable enough to stop and adjust? And most of that just bubbled along beneath the surface, only coming to the top when you suddenly realised it was nearly lunch time, or something bit you, or a smell or sight from the road jolted you. The rest of the time... it was all about just being.

The distances in Zambia were longish but it was mostly on tarmac and the terrain was rolling rather than mountainous. However, tarmac is no guarantee of no punctures and sure enough, a couple of days in, I was tootling along minding my own business, feeling good when suddenly the front wheel started to thunk thunk thunk and my heart sank. I know that after several thousand kilometres and on our seventh country in Africa, I should have been adept at changing my tyres, whipping out my tyre levers, expertly flipping the rubber off, feeling for nails, replacing the inner tube and then squeezing the last bit of tyre onto the rim and hey presto –just a bit of pumping and ready for the off again, but the sad reality is, I have never really got the hang of it. I can do almost everything but it is squeezing the last bit of tyre onto the rim that always defeats me. I think you need thumbs of iron and mine appear to be a bit wobbly.

To make matters worse, the puncture happened just outside a small school, and as I slowed to a stop, the entire school whooped with glee and came running out to inspect me. I was clearly the most entertaining thing that was going to happen that day. I was immediately surrounded by about fifty children all smartly dressed in their uniforms. It is a total mystery how mothers in Africa manage to send their children out in brilliant white shirts when they are often living in mud huts with the only water coming from a well some miles away. Two teachers came up to join the crowd and everyone started giving me useful advice, trying to help me open my bag, take the wheel off and generally making the puncture into an enjoyable communal activity. I knew that my lack of skill was going to disappoint them and shame me, but I grabbed a tyre lever and wielded it trying to look like an expert.

Hallelujah at that moment, my knight in shining armour arrived in the shape of Charles. I telegraphed desperation to him across the heads of the fascinated school children, and being a good Christian, he stopped his bike and took over. He could barely get to the wheel through the clustered heads of the boys and girls, who were most appreciative of his skill but wanted to keep a very close eye on him. I was so grateful. I hung around in the background, handing over implements and thanking my lucky stars that he had rescued me – both from a flat tyre and from abject humiliation.

The day into the Zulu Kraal camp was a longish one. It was 177 kilometres, but with plenty of little ups and downs that made my legs heavy and left me dispirited. I fell prey to coke stop madness and had five that day. My record for the whole Tour and a pretty impressive one. They always helped in the moment but there is a law of diminishing returns. That day the force was not with me, and they ended up delaying me. I spent the day catching up to and falling behind Chris and Andre from the USA and South Africa respectively. By this time, both sported fabulously full beards. Facial hair had become an art form amongst the men on the trip. Luke was my number one choice with his Mexican Porn Star moustachios. Scott sported some rather Edwardian mutton chops. Chris's was like a large furry marmot on the end of his chin and was very soft to the touch – sometimes I would relax in the evening by stroking it. Andre looked like a dashing pirate, and Nick remained resolutely clean shaven even in the roughest of conditions. Back to the coke stops. They didn't really help that day and it stretched out endlessly. My zen state deserted me and the watch seemed to have slowed down. I kept looking at it thinking surely half an hour had passed and it would only be five minutes. I was one of the last in to our camp that night, arriving tired and in a bad temper, only to find that we were squished in to a tiny space and it was going to be hard to find anywhere to pitch my tent. I ended up almost against one of the expedition trucks, which meant I didn't have so far to walk with my stuff, but I was also in the main thoroughfare for folk traipsing in and out with their bags. My guy ropes were almost touching the three tents around me and when I opened my tent flap I was peering directly into someone else's private space. Not my favourite night on the trip.

As always on this adventure though, things changed and our Zambia mando day was a cracker. We started off down and over a big bridge and then there was a big but steady climb followed by a day of rolling hills. On this occasion they worked with me, gathering speed going down and then shooting up and over the top of the next one. There was a satisfying rhythm to it and the day passed quickly with strong legs and a cool breeze. I had started out so early that morning that the racing peloton took quite a long time to catch me and then crash past me. I had stopped for a little break at the top of a hill when they emerged in all their lycra splendour out of a thick mist. They had their heads down, legs pumping, teeth gritted as they flashed past me, a wonderful sight. Slightly less wonderful but very amusing was the next group of riders who were slightly ahead of me. Four of the men had stopped for a pee and had scrambled up a bank together to irrigate the crops. There they were, with their brightly-shirted and shorted backs to me, every move being watched by an enthralled audience of about thirty children.

Our camp that night was in Jehovah School and we were in and beside the football pitch. The local kids all came up and some of the riders started playing ball with them. No language was needed. Dennis was our mando champion that day, putting in a storming performance and after dinner I went up to congratulate him. As I gave him a big, smelly hug, he said,

"Ah Alice, now I am a two time winner today."

The ride into Lusaka, my legs felt like Chris Hoy's and it was fast and easy. I almost caught up with Nick, although I had to pedal like a crazy person to do it, and then joy of joys, passed him as he stopped off for a cigarette break and a fanta. We were in Lusaka for a couple of days and it was quite a culture shock. Modern Africa was definitely upon us and I felt a bit like a bush baby suddenly thrust into the light. There was a huge shopping mall with a cinema, food outlets and lots of things to buy. The cinema made me really happy as I hadn't seen a film in months. A herd of us trooped in and sat down to what was showing. It was "Unknown" with Liam Neeson. In fact, it was absolutely dreadful but the pleasure of sitting in the dark in front of a huge screen made up for everything, and I would have happily sat through it twice. I was back the next day for a Jennifer Anniston epic and it was just as well we left after that or I would have started to run out of options. The group mentality had become very strong by this time, so after our film we all headed out for dinner to the (to us) exotic mall options. This was bad news for the budding couples on the trip, who were trying to enjoy a bit of time alone. We all happily gatecrashed their dates and quashed any notion of romance. Love had blossomed on the trip for quite a few of the riders, some of whom went on to have TdA weddings and even produce the next generation of TdA riders.

Time in Lusaka was very disjointing for me. I loved the cinema, and the mall with all its shops and variety of food but it also jolted me out of my Zambia dream state where it was just me and my bike and the warm air and the bush. It made me feel out of kilter and restless as the old Africa and the new Africa collided. That feeling was to wax and wane as we continued down south, but the feeling that our real worlds from back home were coming closer started to hang over all of us.

Then my two worlds did collide, as I cycled into Livingstone and the Victoria falls to meet my three friends who were coming to meet me and ride the next stage across Botswana with me as sectional riders. Sam, Angela and Amy. I knew Sam and Angela but they didn't know each other and Sam had brought Amy who I had never met before.

Angela and I had met and shared a room and a tent when we did the Trans Atlas Traverse a couple of years before. This is a mountain bike trip across the Atlas Mountains in Morocco and is run by Saddle Skedaddle in the UK and Epic Morocco in Morocco. Little did I know it at the time, but that trip was to have a profound effect on my life and in fact lead to my going to live in Morocco. But that is an entirely different story. Angela and I had bonded over tajines and mint teas. She was a very good rider but preferred road and had got sick on the Morocco trip which meant she had to ride with me, the slowbie, until she got her stomach and bike legs back. I loved her determination, her sense of fun and her positive attitude. She was also doing the Etape so I knew she would be in great shape.

Sam and I had met in Manchester and did lots of outdoor stuff together. We infamously participated in a mountainbike/trail running adventure race in the Lake district. I managed to run for all of about a kilometre before I decided that, not having done any running training at all, this running malarkey was not for me and dropping to a fast walk. I remember looking very enviously at a high-achieving couple, where the man had the woman attached to bungees so that he could pull her along faster. We made a couple of tactical errors too: the first was to go for high points without looking at the contours on the map which would have warned us that even though we would get lots of points if we reached that checkpoint, we would have to climb a vertical waterfall to get there. Our last error was treating our lunch break as just that, a break. We sat down and got out our picnic, munched away and then went to the loo block to wash up and change our shoes and socks to get on to the bikes for the second half of the race. We were oblivious to the fact that the minutes were ticking away and all the other racers were in and out in less than five minutes. Sam even took time to flirt with the checkpoint man, showing him her nice red French manicure at some length. We came last. But we did enjoy it and became friends for, I hope, life. Amy I didn't know at all but was a close friend of Sam's and a good rider.

After suffering heinously in Egypt from the shock of the distances and the relentlessness of it all in the face of a severe lack of training, I phoned Sam from Luxor and left the following message on her answer machine,

"Sam, train, you have to train. You have to get out every weekend and do two long rides back to back. You will die if you don't train. I am on my knees and I still have nine countries to go. If you come and meet us when we are all strong and ridden in and you haven't done much, it will be hell. I am not kidding. You have to get out there, you have to train, you have to train."

Sam told me later that it was the sheer desperation in my voice that convinced her as much as my actual words and she and Amy had trained like demons and arrived in Zambia in peak condition.

I had been looking forward to them coming for weeks and had always had it in my mind as a huge high point of the trip. Having friends share an experience with you is something very precious. It was 151 kms from our camp at the Ruze chalets to the Livingstone Lodge and I covered it in record speed. I was so excited to see them that the adrenaline gave me a massive extra push. I drove the pedals round on the biggest cog and focussed totally on the end point. I shocked all the speedy racers as I rolled into camp early and went to sort out our rooms and wait for the girls.

It was so fantastic and yet so strange to see them. I hadn't realised how much of a mini-life I had built for myself within TdA until that point. They were all so fresh and clean and unbattered, that suddenly I felt absolutely exhausted. Tired in my very bones. Everything, however, is alleviated by the gift of chocolate, new supplies of Lancome face cream and some brand new cycling kit. They had had quite the shopping list. One of my big bars of Lindt I ate immediately and alone. I enjoyed every bite, eating till my teeth ached. One I secreted in my bag to bring out to the acclaim of the Eating Club later on and one I went to give to Dennis. I found him outside his tent and handed it over.

"Alice, you bought me chocolate? Lindt – real chocolate!"

A German living in Switzerland has high chocolate standards and he had been talking about Lindt for much of the journey. He kissed me and then disappeared into his tent, clutching his bar, with a look of lust in his eye, not to be seen for some time.

We had a couple of days off in Livingstone and TdA had arranged a sunset river cruise for us that night with beer and music. We were all high on excitement at the unexpected treat, and the beer and it was the perfect way to introduce the girls to everyone. The men were like bees to a honey pot. New women. Hooray. The two Brams came up and thanked me very profusely for bringing in such attractive additions to the group. I was glad to be able to repay them a little for that push up the hill in Kenya.

Livingstone is, of course, famous for the Victoria Falls and the next day we went off to explore. You can hear them long before you can see them. Water really does roar. Locally it is called "the smoke that thunders," because of the noise and the mist that blows back over the falls like smoke. It is a fully immersive experience. You stand on the edge, looking hundreds of feet down with your heart in your mouth, deafened by the noise and soon soaked to the skin. There were lots of school children there with us, all running around in their wet clothes shrieking with joy. So, we did the same. There are little bridges and paths across lesser falls and lots of opportunities to scare yourself a little. There are also rainbows everywhere, magical prisms flashing in and out of the mists.

We still had a day before we had to get back on the bikes and the girls were getting nervous, understandably so, about the first bit of riding with people who had already got used to the routine. I left them to fettle with their bikes and rested. At the beginning of the race, I had wanted to do lots of sightseeing and exploring on the rest days, but at this stage I realised that I actually needed to stop, to lie down and spend at least some of the days off asleep and recuperating. I felt guilty as my friends had just arrived and were full of energy but I was exhausted and could feel myself being tetchy about getting enough rest on my days off. That last night in Livingstone, we all prepared for the next day, got into bed early and then, far too soon for my liking, the alarm went off and it was time to get out there again.

Sometimes you have days you will never forget. We all woke up with various states of nerves. I always felt nervous getting on the bike after a rest day, but by now it was a pretty mild feeling, whereas for Angela, Sam and Amy it was very much first day at big school proportions. We all set off together on nice terrain. It was tarmac with thick, foresty jungle on either side, so there wasn't much to see. It was going to be a very easy day as we only had 80 kilometres to go. This particular section of the race was the most popular for sectional riders and we had around fifteen new people to get acquainted with. They all looked so fresh and strong with nice, clean, shiny bikes. The whole group was checking each other out a bit like dogs when they first meet, without the bottom sniffing. With my quotient of new, pretty girls, I suddenly had lots of new friends among the male riders,

"Hey, Alice, how's it going? Are these your friends from the UK?........"

We took it nice and easy, there was a pretty relaxed atmosphere as the day was short, we'd just had two days rest, and we were about to enter a new country, Botswana. I was riding along when I saw a concertina of riders up ahead. They were bunching together a bit and stop starting on the road. I cycled on a bit further from Amy and Sam to find out what was going on. Someone from the group in front shouted back,

"There are elephant in the trees."

The first eight years of my life I was brought up in Uganda. We lived in the foothills of the Mountains of the Moon, the Rwenzoris, and down the escarpment to the plains was a magnificent game park. At weekends, Dad would drive us down the red dirt road for family outings to the best zoo in the world. This was the days before Idi Amin and his murdering soldiers went down to that park with their machine guns and managed to annihilate thousands of animals in an orgy of butchery. He butchered hundreds of thousands of people too. That was all in the future however and, happily, we had no notion of that on these incredible drives. The park was teeming with game on a scale that is tragically unimaginable now. Herds of elephant, buffalo, zebra, and antelope all vied for space. Lions were common, and one day when we had stopped the car to watch two buck fighting, a lioness used our car for camouflage and raced out from behind it to make her kill of one of them. Cheetah raced across the grass, quicker than anything I could think of at that age, intent on dinner. It was beautiful and exhilarating but also scary. I understood that animals kill and eat each other and that death is real and bloody.

The most dangerous animal in the African bush is considered to be the buffalo, and you should never get between a hippo and water, but the stories I remember the best are about elephant. My Mum and Dad would talk in those hushed tones, so particularly attractive to a child's ear, about people who had been killed by an elephant. There was one young married couple who had gone down to the park in a smallish car. Somehow, they had enraged the bull of a herd, and he had charged the car time and again. He wrecked it, they couldn't get away, and they were trampled to death, crushed inside their car.

"Never get out of the car, ever, unless I tell you to," Mum would say and it was one instruction that my brother and I always obeyed. If we had to stop for a wee, it was a hurried and harried affair.

I was afraid of elephants.

"There are elephant in the trees," shouted the rider up ahead.

All those childhood tales rushed back to the forefront of my mind and I decided that caution was the better part of valour. I stopped the bike to wait till they had passed. I thought I may as well make the most of my enforced leisure, so I got out my suntan cream to put on a layer. I was rummaging around in the bottom of my bag with my head bent, when I heard a sound that made me jump right into my throat. The trumpet call of an African elephant, an angry African elephant.

A large bull elephant exploded out of the bush just 30 metres away to my left, slightly ahead of me and across the road. His ears were out and flapping, and his trunk was raised. He was trumpeting his rage and charging straight at me. I only had one thought,

"I am going to die."

Instinct took over. I dropped my bag, wrenched my bike round to the opposite direction and slammed down on the pedals. Time kaleidoscoped. It was only seconds but I had time to see and hear and feel everything down to the very last detail and to think. Adrenaline had flooded my body. My legs were pumping up and down, up and down, faster than they ever had before. My heart was beating at double or triple its normal rate, forcing oxygen down into the muscles, even though I could barely breathe. I knew that there was absolutely no way I could outride a charging elephant. They reach speeds of 50 km per hour and he was just thirty metres away from me and closing.

My head was working as furiously as my legs.

"Should I get off the bike and make a run for it into the bush? Maybe I could climb a tree and hide from him."

The trees were thorn trees with five inch thorns which would rip me to pieces, and I would never get up one. I was no speed monster even on the bike and on foot I was a snail. I was wearing bright yellow lycra, which presumably would be like a red rag to a bull.

I kept on pedalling.

He was so close, I could actually feel the ground moving as he pounded down towards me. I could hear the noise of his enormous feet smacking onto the tarmac. In my peripheral vision, I saw the other riders up ahead, all also frantically pedaling in the opposite direction.

I was going to die, I was going to be crushed here on this tarmac road in Africa.

I was so scared. I wondered what it would feel like.

"Pretty damn sore," my inner voice told me.

I kept pushing the pedals. I thought about my family. Should I get off the bike and run? Should I? He was so, so close now. I couldn't go any faster. I did not want to die. I loved life. Would he gore me with those tusks or would he just stamp on me? How long would it take?

"I hope he crushes my head first so I don't feel too much," I thought.

I kept pedalling as fast, as hard as I could. I was still searching for alternatives, but there weren't any. Mentally, I started to curl into myself, like you do in the last moments before a crash.

Then, he stopped. He just stopped. The noise of his feet on the ground and the shudders as he hit the tarmac came to an end. He had seen me off his territory, his job was done.

Relief overwhelmed me. I was ok. I was alive and all in one piece with an unsquashed head and still pedalling like a demon towards my friends. I was SAFE.

If this were a novel, my story would end here, on this incredible high point. But life, unlike the beauty of fiction, has aftermath.

I got back to Sam and the other riders, and I stopped too. I was shaking with the consequences of fear and adrenaline and effort. I couldn't believe it was over.

"Oh my God, are you ok? Look, there it is. Shall we go on? Where's your bag? I can't believe that just happened."

I got off the bike and sat on the roadside for a bit. Time accordioned back to normal. The elephant had crossed over onto the other side and gone into the thick bush. One of the riders in front cycled back with my bag and sunglasses, and told me that Lindsay had got some great photos of me in full flight.

How quickly, we change gear back to having a future. Ten minutes before, I honestly thought I was going to be dead. Now, I was really pleased that he'd taken them and couldn't wait to see them. My heart was back to normal, and I had stopped shaking and was now excited about my mini adventure, already converting it in to a story to impress my niece and nephew with.

Tour D'Afrique: the only thing you have to do is keep going. I got back on the bike. It was time to cross the border into Botswana.

Chapter Eight

Botswana

The trucks and lorries at the Zambia-Botswana border at Kasungulu stretched back for over two kilometres. The border lies along a river at that point and so you need a ferry to get across, hence the enormous queue. The drivers were obviously all used to it and had little camps going. They were clustered in little groups, having lunch or playing cards when we got there. Some were just taking it easy and had stretched out in the shade of their trucks for a siesta.

We got to jump the queue right to the front with the passengers, and walked our bikes on board. Cool air off the river, a seat and a coke that we had bought at one of the little shops on shore, made it a very pleasant trip.

Once on dry land, we only had a few kilometres to go till camp and I spotted a car wash. I had given my bike a quick once over on the rest day but it wasn't clean clean, so I let the girls go on and pulled over to the side. Snake was waiting for me. He was a Botswanan rasta with beautiful dreadlocks and the smile to go with them. I sat and chatted to him while he diligently went over every cog and chain link. A tiny part of me felt guilty at being so lazy but it was defeated by the larger part of me that hates cleaning my bike and was hugely enjoying sitting down and chatting, while someone did it more thoroughly than I ever would. I was not alone in this, all the TDA riders would search out people or places to get their bike cleaned when we were on the road.

We had arrived early so had the chance to go on a game cruise down the Chobi river. We were in an open boat with raised seats, which rocked a bit when the entire TDA team rushed to one side when we spotted anything. We saw hippo and elephants and lots of river birds, dipping and diving for fish. The most beautiful thing for me, though, was the light reflecting on the trees and water making diamond sparkles and perfect shadows.

After dinner, we had our country briefing for Botswana. This stage of TdA is famous for the chances of encountering big game along the road. Because of that, a big game expert had joined the TdA crew and was to stay with us for the whole country, patrolling up and down the road in his jeep. I had imagined someone a bit like Robert Redford in Out of Africa, wearing jodhpurs and a khaki jacket strapped around with belts and bullet holders. Maybe even a pith helmet. As with so many other things in life, I was to be disappointed. Our big game man was very grizzled and not as glamorous as I would have wished for, but he was to give us sound advice.

"Elephants are very dangerous," he said. I nodded vigorously, this chap obviously knew what he was talking about.

"If you come across one on the road, you must stop your bike and turn round and move away until you are at least 100 metres distant from it. Then you just have to wait until s/he crosses the road. If you see a mother with her baby up ahead, keep even further back."

I popped up my hand for a question. " That is all very well but what if you can't see the thing and next minute it is charging out of the bush at you?"

"Pedal like hell!"

Someone else put their hand up. "What if we are cycling along and we come across some lions? Will they hunt us?"

The response was less than reassuring. "I'll be driving up and down the route looking for traces of lion and if we find any, we will pull you all off the route. But if by any slim chance you do meet a lion, retreat cautiously and quietly. But, yes, if it sees you and is hunting, it will go for you and it will get you."

Kasani – Bush Camp, 171 kms. This was our first real day of riding in Botswana. I had changed my cogs, putting a bigger one on the back so that I could get more power going through my legs on the long, flat tarmac roads that characterised this whole stage. Angela, Amy and Sam were all on their light road bikes with tiny tyres. I loved my bike, it had seen me across murderous terrain with barely a complaint, but I was so jealous of their speed and ease. I found myself thinking bitter, bad thoughts which went along the lines of,

"It's all very well for you with your lightweight racing bike and your fresh legs...."

Still, I had the advantage of several thousand kilometres in my legs, and the familiarity with what life on the road was like. We set off together in a mini peloton with Mike, who was an instant hit with everyone.

The day was long and flat and relatively easy for that but we pushed ahead nicely and made good time. I was very proud of my friends as they all rode really well and bravely.

We had excitement when we got to where the camp should have been. It had had to be moved because the big game expert had found lion tracks around it. Now, we felt like we were in the heart of Africa.

I was back in the monster sail tent, as I had lent my other one to Sam and Amy. They went through the rituals of getting the stuff out of the truck, putting up the tent, and getting settled in that I had now got so used to. In Livingstone, with the knowledge that I would be wrestling with the monster tent, I had gone out and bought a big mallet all of my very own and a fearsome cast iron set of proper African tent pegs. What a joy it was at that first bush camp in Botswana not to have to queue for the mallet and to be able to hammer in pegs that didn't immediately bend into Ssss the minute they hit the ground. The monster sail tent actually felt almost secure.

It was strange, though. I felt a bit like a dog with two masters. My current life was TDA: my routines there, my friends there, our group way of thinking and doing things, and now my old life, my "real" life, was thrust violently into the mix with the arrival of my friends. I struggled to reconcile the two, and to make sure I took care and helped them but still had time to be myself, as the Alice I had become, within the TDA family. It also reminded me that this life I was living, would end, that at some point I would have to stop being in Africa, on a bike, under the sky and go back to the UK and a normal life there. I didn't want to think about that. I was still in the middle of it. I couldn't really contemplate the ending.

The riding in Botswana was fast but a bit dull. The chance of seeing animals kept us alert but I did not see a single thing for the whole time we were in the country. Maybe the cycling Gods had decided that I had already had my fair share after my close encounter with an elephant. The tarmac was flat and pretty good, we rode in pelotons and covered big distances. I tended to ride with my friends for part of the day and then break off and have some time on my own. We were at the tail end of the rainy season so had lots of wet weather to contend with. One afternoon, the rainstorm for the day had finished, and the sun had come out strongly. I was pushing the pedals round in a bit of a dream when I started to become aware of a wonderful smell coming from the side of the road. I got off the bike and went to investigate. I was surrounded by small, scrubby bushes of what I think was wild thyme. With every step, I would crush one of the rain-soaked, sun-dried plants and be assaulted by waves of deliciousness. I wonder if that is what it is like for cats with catnip. I did have the urge to roll around in it but a group of riders were not far behind and so I resisted.

On TDA, birthdays were always a cause for celebration. At dinner, a cake would often be produced, cooked goodness knows how without the benefit of an oven, but Kim was a genius. Steve, one of the truck drivers, and an old South African bush hand, also had a secret and cunning way of making cakes in a big pan. Our most special birthday on the trip though, was Christine Wolfe's, as she turned sixty. Christine was a beautiful woman, who also had grace and charm. As the leading racer, her husband, Paul, came in for lots of angst from the other riders. He was a wily old dog, and was racing to win, so was not always popular although I liked him very much, but everyone loved Christine. We were in the grounds of a lodge that night with good camping facilities and very generously, Paul had put money behind the bar. Everyone made an effort and scrubbed up for the celebration. There was music and a cake, all real treats for us. That night produced one of the most memorable photographs of the whole trip. It is of Bastiaan dancing with Christine in her pretty, flowered halter frock. They both have their eyes closed and it shows the love and closeness we felt for each other, bonded together by these experiences we were sharing.

It rained like crazy that night and the monster tent flailed and screamed but stayed upright. Getting up in the dark and mud was never my favourite. I rode with Angela, who was really much stronger than me and was on a road bike and I had to dig deep to keep up, but it was a glorious day. Our camp wasn't though. It was a long dirt road with no good pitching positions, even though we had got in early thanks to Angela's speed. You had a choice: thorns or ants. At the far end of the camp, someone had spotted a big snake in a tree. I chose the pitch furthest away from that tree and kept my tent zipped up very firmly. I moaned about the bush camps but honestly, I think they were my favourite. It was always initially nice when we got to a campsite on this second half of the tour and there were showers and nice grass to pitch on, but the wilder stuff was always better, even if there were snakes and thorns and ants and no water to wash in.

We were heading for Maun, a biggish town, and the stepping off point for trips to the Okavango Delta. It had a bit of a feel of the Wild West to it and a wonderful mixture of rural tribesmen bringing in their cattle to sell in the market and modern shopping malls. A lot of the riders booked to go on small planes to see the herds of animals in the Delta. I didn't and spent time instead wandering around the town and having lunch with my favourite rest day buddy, Nick. We had a Braai in the evening, organised by South African Steve with lots of good barbeque and then songs round the fire. My big fail on this rest day was trying to get my legs waxed. Up in the north of Africa, it was relatively easy but now it was impossible. African women are obviously not at all hairy. Unlike me, I was beginning to resemble a silver-backed gorilla.

As everyone who has just stepped out of the hairdresser's or has ever ridden a bike, knows: wind is the enemy. It has always remained a meteorological mystery to me how the wind can be in your face when you cycle to the shop and then still in your face when you cycle back. Does it just switch round to annoy and slow you down? There is a reason why all top pro-cyclists train in wind tunnels. It is not just the sheer physical effort of pushing yourself through a headwind, it is also the mental anguish of pedalling like crazy and getting nowhere. Many cyclists would much rather go up a big hill than go into a headwind and I think I am one of them, even though I usually start moaning as an incline bites into my legs.

So, what a memorable pleasure it was that first day out of Maun to have a tailwind. You can tell how rare a really good one is by the fact that it was the absolute highlight of the day, perhaps the week. We set off in a big peloton, about twenty of us riding in pairs and made it to the lunch truck by 9.30. It was 80 kms away. The combination of being pushed along by the hands of the wind Gods and the shelter of a peloton made it an easy ride. That must have been why I let myself be talked into the National Team Time Trial that evening by Ruth as we were resting up and eating chocolate before dinner.

This was an annual TDA tradition and as the name suggests, it was a competition to cover an allocated distance in the quickest time in teams of 4 based on nationality. Not only personal honour was at stake, national pride hung in the balance. As you can imagine on a race like TdA, there were some pretty competitive people and add nationalism into the equation and it was always going to get serious... ish.

Ruth and I planned our team based on a number of factors. The pre-requisites were:

1. Being British
2. Being fast
3. Being big/tall so that Ruth and I, who were not fast, could hide behind them in the peloton
4. Being either a girl or a very good looking man
5. If you were a man, having slightly see through cycling shorts so that Ruth and I would be incentivised to bike faster – nb we would be BEHIND the man in question, Ruth asked me to put that in to clarify
6. Having a sense of humour
7. Having access to chocolate or another tasty snack for post race celebrations
8. Being prepared to pump up Ruth and my tyres/change them in case of puncture
9. Being 100% sure of victory against all odds
10. Being a good loser (just in case)

At dinner that night, we surveyed the queue. First choice was Angela, who fit into all the categories except for part two of no4 and all of no5, her shorts were new and hadn't been through the rigours of constant African washing so were still intact and opaque.

Paul Spencer, one of the best racers and in fact number two in the competition until he got malaria, was the next natural choice. He scored highly on all counts but absolutely one hundred percent on part two of no4 and all of no5. His grey cycling shorts had faded to a pale off white and were pretty well completely see through. We approached him just as he was at his most vulnerable, in the dinner queue, hungry and expectant. He said yes and there were high fives all round.

Our team was complete. Or was it? Liam, gold medal winner in the World Championships for Team GB in rowing, his nasty groin abscess all healed up, and another one hundred per center for part two of no4 and all of no5, said he was in too. We weren't sure if this would be allowed as the teams were strictly meant to be four but on application to the race organisers, and after looking at us, they said yes.

I think, they thought we couldn't win. Fortunately, we did not brook that kind of negativity and were sure of victory. We were, admittedly, the only team in the race that featured more than one woman and we were, perhaps, a bit of a long odds bet, but our confidence was high.

After dinner, we were slightly alarmed to see the Dutch team, led by the two Brams, in formation going up and down the road practising their group work and switching. The USA, featuring both top male and female rider of the race, would possibly pose us some problems too. And we felt it was better not to think too much about the German team, who had a look of gritty determination.

Our pre-race preparation consisted of a bit more chocolate and me and Ruth reassuring Paul that we had absolutely NOT chosen him just so as we could leer at his bum in its see through cycling shorts.

The morning of race day dawned. I felt nervous. After all the laughter and joking of the night before, I now had real pre-race jitters. Of course it was ridiculous. We had no chance of winning and no-one would care where we came except for us, but I did not want to be last. Also, I was worried about being shown up in front of the others. Angela, Paul and Liam were all stonkingly good riders and Ruth had the heart of a lion.

We rolled up to the start line. We had 40km ahead of us. That may not seem far, but I knew that I would be cycling above my limit the whole way and I had to take a few very deep breaths to calm myself. I also inwardly and in fact, outwardly, cursed Ruth for suggesting it in the first place. It would be so much easier to just pootle along with the others and enjoy the spectacle.

But here we were and then it was time and off we went. Immediately, I was on the biggest cog, pumping away as hard as I could. Our race plan was very simple. The three faster, stronger riders would go at the front, and Ruth and I would tuck in behind them and cling on. This wasn't great cycling etiquette but it was practical. The reality was that there was no way we were strong enough to keep up any kind of decent race pace if we were bearing the brunt at the head of the group.

Team spirit was very high. A little bit of singing, a couple of jokes, and of course, the see through cycling shorts. Ruth and I fought viciously over who would tuck in behind Paul. But I was still working as hard as I could. Just to keep up, I had to focus and bring out some reserves I didn't know I had.

The kilometres sped by. No time for dreaming or lapsing into my Africa daze. And then – we saw the finish line and the flags up ahead, put in an extra push and collapsed over the line. Euphoria! We had done it. It was amazing. Nerves were nothing. Let's do it again. High fives, sweaty group hugs and a lot of self congratulation. I honestly felt like a champion.

Then we waited anxiously for the results... we had done it in a very respectable 1 hour and 15 minutes and were absolutely not last – in fact we were joint third from the bottom. Job done. That night as I went in to the truck to get my stuff out of the locker, I heard Paul Spencer saying to Scott,

"Ruth and Alice only asked me to be in the team because they wanted to look at my arse...."

Elephant Highway Mando Day wasn't going to be difficult in terms of climbing or being on the dirt but it was very long – 207 km – longer than any day's riding I had done before. Me and my On-One mountain bike were not totally convinced that doing this distance on fat tyres on pavement was a good idea, but nevertheless off we set.

The routine followed its usual path. Me, Sam, Amy and Mike got on the road about 6.30 after a good breakfast. The sun was coming up but it was pretty misty, really reminding me of home in Autumn. Angela was going separately as she had a faster pace.

The four of us rode on at about 23km/hr for 45 minutes or so and then the rain started hammering down. We were all soaked within minutes but at least it wasn't freezing cold. And really, when you know you are going to be on the bike for at least 9 hours, there is no point even thinking about it because there is nothing you can do.

About half an hour later, a big peloton came past and we hopped on the back. It was going about 32km/hr so would pull us to lunch really quickly. This one was a strange mixture of erstwhile racers and speedies like the Brams and Bastiaan and then us. The rain was still hammering down, so hanging on to the wheel in front meant getting a constant faceful of spray. After about twenty minutes, I had had enough. I was having to try too hard to keep up and was worrying that if there was a sudden halt I would go straight into Daniel, who was the wheel in front of me. So, I dropped off and left Amy and Mike to it – Sam had gone a bit before, muttering imprecations.

Congratulating myself on the fact that I would now have a nicer ride, if a slower one, I kept on at about 25km/hr. The next landmark for me would be the lunch truck at 79km. Always something to look forward to, not just because of lunch but because it meant you had achieved a chunk of the day.

The scenery was the usual Botswana fare, dead flat, scrub trees on both sides, cows and a great sky. None of the big game promised but I still kept a look out for elephant, giraffe and lions. By now, the rain had eased off but it was dull and overcast.

By 10 am I was getting really hungry and no sign of lunch, also weirdly no-one had passed me for a while and I was expecting both Nick and Christine to have overtaken.

Anyway, I pushed on. Upped my gears and the pace a bit as the hunger pangs gnawed. By 1030, I decided to stop and check the route instructions on my camera – maybe the lunch truck was at 89? Checked them – no – there it was, 79. So, upped the pace again and on I went. At 11 am, I realised that something was really wrong. Even if I had been doing about 15km/hr I would have hit it by now. So I got the camera out, checked again, and saw the fatal words,

"Right turn at Namibia sign, 47km"

This was not a good moment in my life. I had missed the only turn on the route and done roughly an extra 60km out of my way on the longest ride day of the Tour. It was raining again and I only had two PVM bars and a coke in my bag.

But you can never tell how you will react to these things. Bizarrely, instead of ranting and throwing my bike to the ground and kicking a tree, I was actually pretty cheerful and just turned round (into a headwind obviously) and started back.

Two hours later, the lunch truck found me. When I hadn't turned up by the time the sweep came in, they worked out what I had done and had both saved me loads of food – thank you Gabe and Claire – and come back to get me.

Now I had some choices. The mando distance was 207km and although I had buggered up the route monumentally, I still had the option to do at least that distance. The question was should I just go back to camp in the truck having done about 147km, should I go to the refresh stop and do the last 50km which would leave me just shy of the mando distance, or should I get dropped off by the truck when we caught up with the sweep and do as much as I could. I chose the last option – fuelled by a desire to do the distance and also the vast quantity of cheese sandwiches I had just consumed.

We caught up with Nick, the sweep and also our race director, with 90km to go. I got out and started cycling as hard as I could to see if I could get to any of the other riders. About 3/4s of an hour later, Ram, Phil, Ribka and Aman rolled into view standing under a tree. Ribka was waiting for the truck as her knee had gone but Phil and Ram were ready to roll on. Joy! A petit peleton and company for the last 70km. By now I was absolutely determined to make it... Phil was tall and slim and had a very distinct upright posture on the bike. He was a very reliable, solid rider, not usually the fastest but a finisher. Ram was crazed and beautiful. He had loads of natural talent on the bike and was young and fit but he was way too interested in everything going on around him to race, and wanted to take in every experience. He also had a massive stash of PVM bars which he carried on the bike with him, even though they weighed about 3 kg. From the ultimately desirable chocolate and strawberry, to the less fabulous banana, he had them all. This was going to prove useful.

Our fabulous three cracked on. We got to the refresh stop where Martin the mechanic and Brian from TDA were waiting for us. Brian warned us that unless we did at least 28km/hr for the last 60km he would sweep us up in the truck. We had to make the border crossing into Namibia by 6pm.

Martin joined us, and the four of us formed up and decided to do 1km pulls at the front. It was sore but it worked like a dream. We all pushed, dropping out if a pee break or flat occurred and then catching again. I was on fire, cycling like the demons of hell were after me, and keeping up a manic pace. I had pulled a bit ahead and was on my own at about 15km from the border when hunger struck. I stopped and stuffed down a cheese sandwich, saved from the truck, and the others caught up. We plundered Ram's PVM stash, sometimes a cheese sandwich is just not enough, and on we went.

The story has a happy ending. At almost exactly 6pm we hit the border crossing. We had made it. We collapsed off the bikes, high-fived all round and indulged in an orgy of self-congratulation. We were the last riders in that day but we had really blasted that last 70km and we felt fantastic.

Of course when we got to camp, I was roundly and rightly mocked for missing the one and only turn of the day. Fortunately, I didn't have much of a reputation to lose. I worked out that all in all, I had done around an extra 25km over the 207km distance, and I had had one of my best days of the Tour.

Another country done. It seemed almost inconceivable, but we just had two left.

Chapter Nine

Namibia

First day into Namibia and I was still enjoying my celebratory status as "missed the only turning in Botswana" Morrison. Namibia was going to be back to some more interesting and varied riding: on road and off road, hills, plains, big distances, rain and mud and the famous sand dunes.

Border crossings always mean change but in this case, the weather looked set to stay pretty much the same. Dark clouds in the morning boded rain later on. The South Africa effect could be felt even more keenly in Namibia as we approached the economic giant of Africa. Our midday stop on that first day was in Gobabi. It was a pleasant small town, with a shop-lined high street and a famous German bakery. Mike and I had spent the entire morning discussing what we would eat there and what the best German cakes were. You would think that all that talk of carbs would have speeded us up and given power to our legs, but, sadly no, and our lack of performance was to have dire consequences. When, we got to the German Bakery, we had to wade through dozens of bikes to the door, not a good sign. Inside, there was a sea of TdA riders, and no cakes. No cakes. The locusts had got there before us and cleaned out the shelves. No apple strudel, no black forest gateau, not even a scone. We were devastated. I felt violence welling within me when one rider proudly told me that he had had three helping of apple pie with cream. I smiled but inwardly wished him clogged arteries and an early death from heart disease.

Fortunately, there was a big supermarket a little further on. Mike and I decided we would have doughnuts and went in to search out the most gooey concoction we could find. One jam-filled, pink-iced bun later and a coke of course and we were ready to go again. That is when I spotted it.

ALICE TURN HERE!

A massive sign with huge black letters and arrows pointing right, decorated with TDA orange direction ribbon and almost obscuring a stop sign. Chris Fenar and Kristiaan had spent their morning profitably, making sure I wouldn't go wrong again. I laughed all the way up the next hill.

By this time, the clouds weren't just dark, they were black and the light had gone dusky. It looked like serious rain was coming. Mike, who doesn't like rain, decided to turn back into town to wait it out but I was on it and wanted to keep going. I put my rain jacket on, left the town behind and started up a big hill. Suddenly, there was a clap of thunder, the clouds burst and hail stones the size of pigeon eggs rattled out of the sky. They were smashing against me and stinging my bare legs and face. I flung the bike to the side of the road and ran towards the nearest shelter. It wasn't great, a scabby thorn tree, but I huddled as close as I could get to the trunk. The violence of the storm was shocking. The hail bounced back off the road and was coming down so thick and fast that I could barely see twenty metres ahead of me.

"Mike is a very wise man," I thought to myself as I pictured him sitting in a cafe somewhere having a coffee. As soon as it had started, the hail was over and I could escape from my thorny nest back on to the bike.

The countries were going by so fast now that it was scary. Soon, the TdA bubble was going to be burst. How could it possibly be that I had already cycled through eight countries in Africa? Every day was filled with new sensations and new experiences but bounded by a rigid and comforting routine. I didn't have to struggle with motivation or discipline or choices, none of us did. There was only one thing we had to do all day and that was get on the bike and ride. This was the most fantastically liberating feeling. No work, no family, no friends, no TV, no radio, no shopping... all things I love and missed, but being away from them all, gives you the opportunity to rethink yourself and to just enjoy the moment. Free from all distractions. Untrameled.

Of course, there were still all of the daily perturbations that are part of the human condition. I discovered, or rather confirmed, that nothing spurs me on like a bit of of good old fashioned hatred. I would manufacture a small grudge against a fellow rider and then use that to help me catch them up and leave them crushed in my wake, riding on feeling ridiculously victorious. I used a very convenient and arbitrary set of selection criteria. None of the racers ever came into my ambit, only people I could actually physically compete with.

There is a lot of etiquette to riding, especially if you are in a group. Apart from the obvious things like, "don't cause a fellow rider to crash", the main one is not to steal someone else's shelter. When you are riding in a peloton or close group, the person or people at the front take the brunt of pushing through the air resistance. This means that when you are behind them, you are sheltered and it takes less energy to cycle. You have to cling close to their wheel and manners demand that you then take a shot at the front and they get to cycle behind you.

Mike, with my eternal gratitude, had taken a couple of long days in Egypt when we were riding together when he took the front almost all the time, because I was so much less strong than he was and I was suffering. I always offered to come up to the front, and then rained blessings down on his head when he refused.

There was one member of TDA, though, who was notorious for creeping up behind you and then sitting on your back wheel and stealing your shelter without ever taking a turn at the front. On one of those first days in Namibia, Nick and I were cycling up a slow but long drag chatting away when suddenly my bike felt heavier. We looked behind us and there was our shadow. Nick, alpha male, standing for no nonsense, looked across at me, smiled and then slowed his pace down to an almost stop. Then he speeded up, then he slowed down. There was swearing from behind. Our grins grew. Objective achieved, our shadow overtook us, muttering imprecations and cycled off into the distance under his own steam while we stopped for a fag break (Nick) and a mild bitch (both of us).

Nick pushed on and I was left on my own under the blue sky. It was turning into a perfect day. A few kilometres later, I got to have one of those rare and precious Africa moments when I got off the bike, lay down in the grass and just enjoyed being. I had some honeyed popcorn, the birds were singing, and the sun was warm.

Witvei to Windhoek, the last stage of the Elephant Highway, and the last ride with my three friends from the UK. It was 159 kilometres of girlie peloton. We were riding into a rest day, the end of the girls' trip and a planned big night out in Windhoek so we were all giddy. The morning whizzed by and the lunch truck honed into view. We were feeling strong and confident and full of sandwiches, and so, of course, God looked down from on high and threw us a strong headwind, very sticky tarmac and nasty, draggy hills. The next 30 km was horrible. The giddiness morphed into grim determination and we just ploughed on, heads down. Things perked up for the last section coming into Windhoek as the scenery got a little bit more interesting and the hills started to face down rather than up and then there we were, at camp. Amy, Angela and Sam were there. They had done it! Cycled a section of the Tour D'Afrique and had the thigh muscles, bites and crazy tanlines to prove it.

All of us dispersed to our various hotels to get ready for out big night out in civilization. Food was obviously the main concern and the boys were unanimous in where we should go: Joe's Beerhouse. Do you think it was the name that attracted them? Joe's has big scrubbed down wooden tables with benches on each side, candles in bottles, nick knacks in every nook and cranny and a lot of beer. It also serves "wholesome Namibian and German food" which translates into huge portions of fresh meat. Protein hungry, we salivated over a menu of curried bobotie (South African dish of minced meat)of game, springbok skewers, pork knuckle, ladies' eisban (small pork knuckle), oryx fillet. ... you get the idea.

I settled for Zebra steak with a slight twinge of guilt, and lion's paw chocolate brownie for dessert. Huge mounds of food arrived, enough to sate the appetites of even the hungriest rider and then we were ready to hit the town.

The difficulty of trying to get a disparate group of people moving in the same direction in a strange town should not be underestimated. We were heading for a club called Zanzibar and eventually about 15 of us crammed into a minibus. I was perched on Big Bram's knee and spent the journey alternately worrying about squashing him and enjoying being perched on Big Bram.

I hadn't been out dancing since the shoulder shaking of Ethiopia. It was all a lot more familiar in Zanzibar. It could have been a club in Camden except with more African music. It was fun, the people were laid back and the music was good.

I woke up in my lovely hotel room the next morning with a strange feeling. Suddenly, from nowhere, I knew that I just could not go on. This was a rest day but the next day was back on the bike and my mind, soul and body were united. No, we can't do it. We need a rest. It was a crisis that came out of the blue. I wasn't ill or injured. Nothing in particular had happened to cause it, but I had had enough. I tried to work out what it was that made me want to stop at that particular moment when I was strong and everything had got so much easier. It didn't really make sense. I had flogged myself almost to death through the heat and ruts of Sudan, powered through the mud and flies of Tanzania and dragged myself up the mountains of Ethiopia, so why now? I didn't really have an answer.

Psychologically, I think a factor was the wonderful disruption of having friends with me for a couple of weeks, bringing the real world into my TdA bubble. They reminded me that it was soon going to be over. I had snapped horribly at Angela one day when she mentioned this. Telling her that after all we still had two countries left out of the ten, a fifth still to go, but she was right, it was soon going to be over.

Physically, of course, although I felt strong, I was physically tired. It had been relentless for three months. I had put my body through something which it had never even come close to experiencing before.

The biggest factor though was mental strength, or in this case weakness. Every time I had had to force myself back on the bike and finish a long day some of my mental resilience had been used up. Every time I had had to wait at the end of the queue for dinner or the bike shop or the medical tent, I had exhausted some patience. Every time I had had to push through feeling weak or not good enough or not fast enough or not strong enough I had spent some of my emotional reserves. I had withdrawn too much. The bank was empty.

I knew that Nick would be open to corruption, so catching him at a weak moment at breakfast, I asked if he would play truant with me, stay an extra couple of days in Windhoek and then catch up with the others at Sossus Vlei. He agreed. The three days of rest stretched ahead from the lovely confines of the Thule hotel, set high in the hills above the city.

First, though, I had to go to camp, let them know what we were doing and also make sure our bikes got put on the trucks so that they would be waiting for us in Sossusvlei. In camp, I got nabbed by a couple of media people who wanted to get some comment for programmes they were doing. The first was pretty standard, a local television station was covering the colourful lycra progress of TdA through the country and just wanted some generic comments which I was really happy to give. The second was much more complex. I was confronted by a young and earnest German man, who if he did not have a beard and glasses, certainly should have.

"So, how does TdA support the empowerment of women in Africa?" was his opening gambit. Cranking my brain in to gear, I began what I thought was a rather nice soundbite on how we were riding in exactly the same conditions as the men and competing on entirely equal terms. He was not as impressed with this as I was.

"Yes, but how does that help African women to become more emancipated? I am doing a programme on women in Africa and their empowerment."

I cast around for something useful I could give him, not wanting to disappoint someone who was clearly so well-meaning.

The best I could do was to outline some of the things that happened during the ride, the conversations we had with local women, the example we set as women doing something so difficult on equal terms with our male co-riders, the local women riders who joined us in Ethiopia, and the money we brought into the local economy as we rode through, which would be of benefit to women and their families.

It was a good question though, not necessarily the specific one of what were we doing to empower women, but were we doing anything that contributed towards the countries that we were cycling through and should we be?

The answer was yes but within limits. For each TdA rider, a bicycle was donated by the Tour D'Afrique company to medical workers in remote areas to help them get to their patients more easily. TdA encouraged local riders to take part in stages that went across their country, and hosted them for free. All our food was bought locally as we travelled through. This was all at the company level. In addition, we were all spending our tourist dollars on extra food, hotel rooms, meals and souvenirs and of course, many of the riders were raising money for charity, although not all for African charities.

The other thing that we all did on a personal level was to try and keep a light footprint. Everyone was diligent about recycling where possible and not littering. Most of the riders made a real effort to be courteous and open to conversations with people as we met them on the road – although there was the occasional moment in cafes and restaurants when I blushed for us all as hunger trumped politeness.

The thing that I most enjoyed doing was learning a bit of the local language in every country that we passed through. I did it for pleasure and because I like languages but also to show respect to the people of that country and not just to assume that they should all speak English or French. This was easy peasy in the Arabic countries, where I had the head start of an Arabic degree, and we were in Ethiopia for long enough for my Amharic to come along quite nicely, helped by Aman and Ribka. In other countries, it really was just 20 – 30 words so that I could greet people and say please and thank you. I tried to learn at least one new word a day and then use it till I remembered it. Here is my list of homework words from a couple of days into our Malawi ride – where 57% of the people speak Chichewa. I had obviously got the greetings down already and was trying to move conversations on. Clearly, I was a bit ambitious with "God", I never got fluent enough in Chichewa to get metaphysical.

Munthu – person

Bwenzi – friend

Mulungu – God

Mvula – rain

Ulendo – journey

Hema – tent

Mukv pita kuti – where are you going?

Nidv pita Lilongwe – I am going to Lilongwe

Whether the words were spelt or pronounced correctly, or even meant what I thought they did, I never really knew. What I did know was that every time I stumbled through some words or phrases in a national language, I was greeted with absolute delight. These tiny interactions were like gold nuggets. We share so much as human beings, and have so much more in common than we have that divides us.

It was slightly weird after the trucks had left with the cavalcade and it was just Nick and me enjoying the sights of Windhoek, but good weird. The three days were a kind of pause for me and a reset. I had to accept that whether I wanted it to or not, this trip was going to end and I was going to have to get back to "real" life. I also had to gird my loins for the next part of the trip, given I was absolutely knackered.

So, how did I go about this? Watched the Royal Wedding on the telly in my room of course. It was great lying there, munching on Dairy Milk and, yes, even getting a tear in my eye as I watched them walk down the aisle and say their vows. I waved my metaphorical Union Jack and suddenly the thought of going back didn't seem quite so bad.

It was great to lounge around. Especially as Windhoek was very developed and had all the comforts of home and our hotel was gorgeous, set up on the hilltops looking over the city, with a permanent breeze. We walked down into town and watched Thor, which since it was directed by Kenneth Brannagh, I had high hopes for but they were dashed. I was still in love with the novelty of being in a cinema again, though, so enjoyed it nevertheless. Walking back up the hill, my legs started to hurt and I felt a surge of pride. I had clearly arrived as a cyclist. I could now count myself amongst the elites who claim to spend most of the time that they are not on their bikes, lying down and who will not walk upstairs because it is bad for their cycling legs.

The other thing I did in my time out, was start applying for jobs. I had nothing to go back to in the UK and so it was time to start seeing what might be out there. I had worked at Vision and Media for nine years and I had got that job through the Guardian Media page. In the intervening years, everything had totally changed and moved online, which was a big advantage as I could access all the opportunities from a nice cafe in Windhoek. My head wasn't really in the game because I didn't want to go back to work, but I forced myself and sat down to search out some opportunities. I applied for CEO of a large hospital in the northwest of England, a post I had very few (no?) qualifications for and then spent a few hours happily spending the salary. I also applied for a job as Head of News for a South African

Broadcaster, a job I had arguably a few more qualifications for. Then I spent a few hours imagining myself transforming the African Broadcast Industry.

I didn't get the jobs.

We had hired a car and a driver to take us up to Sossusvlei to rejoin the group and set off at a good hour. It would have been easier on a bike. Torrential flooding had nearly destroyed the road and the car was sliding on the ice rink of mud. Nick and the driver spent as much time outside the car trying to push it out of giant lakes in the middle of the road as they did in it. A couple of hours into the journey, we slowed and slowed and stopped. Bonnet up, there was lots of looking and prodding at engine parts and it transpired that we had sprung an oil leak. We were in the middle of nowhere but fortunately there was phone reception. They had to send another car out for us, so we sat by the edge of the road and waited. I took lots of pictures of ants.

Sossusvlei is at the edge of the red dunes which are such an intrinsic part of Namibia's reputation as one of the most beautiful countries in Africa. They are truly magnificent. I had been a bit snooty about them before I got there. I reckoned that a childhood spent partly in the Arabian Gulf and several trips across the Western Desert in Egypt meant I had seen just about all the dunes I needed to. But I was wrong. Perfect curves of gold, amber and red stretching out further than I could see and set off by the bluest of skies. The air was completely still and quite cool. You could roll down them, jump like a maniac or sit and enjoy the quiet. The light was clear in the morning and then made the sand glow as we got closer to noon, casting sharp shadows.

Our bikes had got covered in mud and dust on their journey on top of the trucks so it was time for some TLC and also to change my chain ring back to normal size at the back. We were heading for a lot of off road, some mud and some hills, so I wouldn't be able to keep on pushing the bad boy I had put on for Botswana.

Back on the road with Mike and 139km to go. We set of with our morning mantra, " Morgenstund hat gold im mund" It was a lovely morning, but it was a nasty reintroduction to the bike. Corrugated track made a comeback, combined with a heavy headwind. The corrugation and the wind lasted all morning, right up to the lunch truck. But I forgave all of it because of the surroundings. We were cycling through endless green grasslands. The rains had been good that year so they were especially lush and were dancing in the wind. We saw springbok, gazelles and even a couple of kudu (type of antelope) moving gracefully across the plain and stopping to graze. In the background was a line of fairytale mountains.

I was loving the scenery but I felt like I had slowed down. This was my diary entry for our next Mando day which was 153 km from Betta to Konkeip Lapa.

"Had a flat when I got to the bike. Miserable. Left camp at quarter to seven and set off for another mammoth ride. Dirt, corrugation, scenery like yesterday, sand. Took me 4 ½ hours to get to the lunch truck again – too long. Hill just before lunch – big pass. Lunch truck seemed to take forever and ever. After lunch it was much better. Rode alone all day. Got into camp at 4 pm and put tent up. DID IT! Puncture fixed by Bob and co."

That night, the rain poured down without stopping. Little puddles punctuated my ground sheet but I was dry and cosy in the sleeping bag. It was still going strong at breakfast but there was no help for it, on to the bike. At least I didn't have a flat. I set off nice and promptly at 6.30 and got a shock as I tried to cycle up the hill. The road was sticky toffee mud. I had to put my feet down as I slurped through it to a halt. The rain kept coming down. Up at the top of the bank, there was a straight caramel coloured road ahead. The wheels felt like they were superglued to the road, my thighs were burning within five minutes. Within twenty minutes, I was panting like a Labrador in the Bahamas. It was still pouring down. I didn't know quite what tactic to go for. Should I keep in a heavy gear and just power on through, or should I try and up the cadence a bit. Scott, went past me yelling,

Get out of that gear, Alice, you are way too high!" I had my answer. Even though I shifted down, my speed didn't shift up.

Then I heard a horn blaring, some road hog had his hand right down. I looked over my shoulder and there was one of our trucks bearing down on me, horn going like crazy, with Ferdi leaning out the window yelling,

"Get off the road, get off the road," in slightly panic stricken tones. The truck was going at full pelt and since it was much bigger than me, I obeyed and flung myself into a ditch. I found out in camp that they had to go that fast to get through the mud, and they had no real steering, so they hammered down the road scattering riders as they went.

Back on, I spotted a possible advantage, the truck had left deep grooves in the road, which weren't quite as hard to cycle in. Result! Well, result for about ten minutes until they filled with water and then it was like biking through a swimming pool. It was still raining. By now, there were only a very few of us left biking and it was getting to be really fun. We were covered in filth, our legs were burning and we were going at a snail's pace, but it was a shared effort and we were out there in the middle of Africa, not sitting behind a computer in an office.

31 kms of rain, sweat and tears and then it was over and we were in a small town and on tarmac. It was still raining. The survivors of the mud track, all gathered in a little cafe where God proved that he existed by providing us with hot pies, freshly baked. We ate through the first batch and then we waited and ate through the next batch. I do not think that life will ever provide me with a bigger treat. We shared them with laughter and the pure camaraderie you can only earn through difficulty. Me, Carrie, Tori, Pretty Peter, Kim, Andre and Charles.

I pushed on and slogged into a cross wind for the rest of the day, but cycled hard and that day I was first lady back at camp.

Mando day in Namibia. By now I was madly in love with the country, besotted by its supermodel beauty. Our day was 170 km from Hubas Camp to Felix Unite on the Orange River. It was going to be really varied: off road, hilly, tarmac, through a couple of gorges and a little bit of desert. I was off and out by 6.15 am as the sun was rising. The landscape had changed from the silvery green grasslands to a golden moorland. The light was luminous, making everything glow. Our first challenge was a big mountain pass, which led into a deep canyon on our left. Three delicate springbok sprang out of the scrubland with their leggy gait and bounced in front of me. My legs felt great and I was going easily and well, it was one of those hills that you could get a good rhythm on and the surface was smooth not sticky. A lot of the time, I am cycling through fatigue and pain which makes these moments of grace when everything comes together and you feel all-powerful so much the sweeter.

Because, I had set off so early and had made good time, I rolled into lunch as first lady and was happy about the day. However, nothing invites calamity so quickly as a smidgeon of smugness. I sometimes think God is sitting up in heaven with an army of angels whose only job it is, is to search out self congratulation and punish it mercilessly. I started after lunch for an offroad section up a big sandy hill and it all began to go horribly wrong.

A sound like the gnashing of a demon's teeth issued from my derailleur and chain rings. I ignored it. It got louder, two demon decibels. I ignored it. The chain started slipping and catching on every third or fourth revolution. I ignored it. The reason for my determined placing of my head in the metaphorical sand was simple. I do not know anything at all about bike, or any other, mechanics. I have a blindness for it that is both embarrassing and inexplicable. In fact, I am very badly gifted by nature to be an Adventurer because I possess neither technical aptitude nor a sense of direction. Fortunately, I do have a sense of the ridiculous. So, I knew that whatever was wrong with my trusty steed, I was in the middle of Mando day, on my own, approaching the Namibian desert, and there was absolutely nothing I could do about it.

Then the chain came off.

For the next hour, I struggled on. The chain stuck or came off around every five minutes and the sounds my poor bike was making were very distressing, but I didn't know what else to do and I wanted to finish the day, so I just kept going.

Fortunately, I then hit a downhill into the deserty, sand section and I could freewheel. I was praying all the while that the bike would just hold out till I could get to Felix Unite and put it in the safe hands of Martin and Gabe. God had clearly turned his earpiece off though, because 20 minutes later when the downhill stopped and I had to pedal again, the chain froze completely and that was it.

I was on my own, in the middle of a desert in the middle of nowhere, and my bike wasn't working. I got off, sat down on a stone and took out a power bar, Strawberry and chocolate, my favourite. I didn't have long to wait before I saw the cavalry in the distance: Tori and Carrie, Kim and Peter. Saved!

By this stage of the trip, things were getting tribal and Tori had started to decorate her bike in a way that would have done the Wildlings of Game of Thrones proud. She had an antelope skull tied to her handlebars with a much-abused Barbie stuffed into the eye sockets.

They all leaped off their bikes and came to fettle. Bike tools were produced, there was screwing and unscrewing and muttering and head shaking. I looked on and nodded a lot. Kim stripped down to his bib and shorts and did press ups in the sand.

"It's your jockey wheel," said Tori.

"Ahh," said I.

Using the equivalent of a Blue Peter empty milk carton and some sticky back plastic, she fixed it well enough to last through the next few kilometres, but warned me to be gentle. The posse then rode off and disappeared into the distance and I followed gingerly. The kilometres passed with gentle pedalling and mild but increasing complaint from my jockey wheel. I knew there was nothing to do except for keep going, but I mulled over all the possibilities endlessly. My only fixed point was that I was determined to finish the day even if I had to walk the last 60km.

Then, a strange sight up ahead on the empty track. Two women, totally naked except for helmets, gloves and cycling shoes, had drawn their bikes across the road and were blocking my path. Tori and Carrie, doing the naked mile.

The Naked Mile. This had been the subject of much discussion for the last few days. It is a tradition on Tour D'Afrique that on the chosen day, all those riders brave enough, ride a naked mile.

"Are you going to do it? Come on, don't be a wimp/pussy/wuss......" had been the dinner refrain. Some people had really good answers, notably Nick.

"I'll do it if Sharita does," was his offer. To be honest, I think we would ALL have done it, if Sharita had but she was not having any of it.

So, here, I was, with our two alpha females in all their glory, blocking my path and demanding I get my kit off. Now, I am Scottish. Public nakedness is not in my genes. I thought of both my Grannies spinning in their grave. I thought back to going to a mixed German sauna when I was 16 – scarred me for life – I thought about social media and a picture of me in the buff on the bike being picked up by Buzz Feed.

"No, way!" All the cajoling was in vain. I couldn't do it, not even for Tori and Carrie. It was way too far out of my comfort zone. My brave North American friends left me to my bah humbug and cycled off into the distance. I had a fantastic view of bottoms wobbling over the potholes and boobs swinging from side to side in time with the pedals. I had to get off the bike I was laughing so hard. Even better, as the girls got further on, they started to hit traffic. I watched as one car after another ground to a halt and men with eyes as big as saucers leaped out to get a better look. There were whoops and whistles and one guy turned his car right round to drive past for another eyeful. It was absolutely hilarious and absolutely brilliant and I laughed till the tears ran down my face.

I had finally got to the TdA refresh stop. They had put one in because it was such a long day with no local stops around till that point and joy of joys they had bought coke for us all. My bike was on its last wheels. Red-haired Christine was at the coke stop too and she had actually abandoned the day and was riding the truck. She offered to lend me her bike to finish the ride. Fantastic. Now I knew I could do it.

I hopped on, got myself used to the different geometry and gears and then put my foot down, charging through the inevitable headwind and perky little hills. Felix Unite in the distance, spread out along the wide, glittery river and Nick had gone on ahead and got me a room overlooking the water. A happy end to a wonderful day.

Chapter Ten

South Africa

Now, there was no avoiding it. We crossed the border into South Africa, left glorious Namibia behind us and we were on the final countdown. Every morning, the sadistic TdA team played the song, (The Final Countdown by Europe) and every morning we all sang or shouted along. That song will probably be the last thing I hear in my head on my deathbed.

So, it was with definitely mixed emotions that I approached our last few days and our ride through South Africa.

With that uncanny border change thing that goes on, the minute we set wheel in our new country, the weather changed. Cold and misty and positively Scottish, even that was preparing us for home. The countryside was pretty with rolling hills and tarmac, although because I hadn't changed my tyres, I had the joy of 140km of sticking to the pavement. It reminded me a little bit of our first days in the Sinai. I guess everything always comes full circle.

Our South African riders were delighted to be home and on their own territory. South African flags got strapped to handlebars, accents thickened, and our riders' briefing had lots of extra information and interruptions.

That last week was bitter sweet. We still had the same job to do, the same miles to cover, but all of us had started to look to the end. When we had set off, our dinner talk had all been getting to know you stuff: where we came from, what we did, how much riding we had done and so on. There had been the inevitable jostling for personality of the camp, and alpha positions. Friendships and alliances were formed. As we continued, we all relaxed and got comfortable with each other. Then, we talked of everything from the day's riding and anecdotes, to geo-politics with Aman and Nick, philosophy and the meaning of life with my biking partner, Mike, and Christianity and faith with Charles, a man with a shining soul. Oh yes, and I almost forgot, how good our boy bikers looked in their lycra with Ribka, Ruth and Marelie.

The South Africa effect was fully upon us and all our camping sites were great. No more having to tie the tent to a toilet to stop it blowing away, or clearing the cow dung off your particular patch before you put your groundsheet down. Lush grass, clean toilet blocks and even ground made everything a lot easier.

My second day in, I woke up with a heavy feeling on my chest, blocked ears and weepy eyes. A full on head cold. I have been blessed with an ox-like constitution and had only got sick a few times on our journey. On the whole, I had felt healthy and strong. Tired, yes. Bunged up, yes. Itchy from all the Tsetse bites on my bottom, yes. But rarely sick. Colds are my Achilles heel, though. I hate them and I am scared of them because they always go to my chest, and I end up with green pus filling my lungs and refusing to budge. So, I was sorry for myself and miserable. The mist was all-encompassing as we rode off, filling the valleys with cotton wool and freezing us unacclimatized riders. I could feel the wetness of it chilling my skin. If it had been a ride in the Peak District, I would probably have hailed it as a wonderful day but here, I had to stop and put all my extra layers on.

"You have to keep your knees warm," said Paul Wolfe, our male champion, "Or you'll get problems." I put another layer on. Advice from Paul Wolfe had to be taken seriously.

Two longish days on the tarmac, not feeling well but without too much challenge on the bike. It was all doable. The evenings were fun though. We were riding down the Western Cape and every little town had a bar or a coffee shop to go to in the evenings. Chocolates and doughnuts were universally available, which wasn't necessarily a good thing as I knew that when I got home I was going to have to severely cut down on the eating or I would pile on the pounds. Being of an optimistic nature, I was sure I would be able to and in fact I thought I might lose weight once I stopped eating African portions and was back to normality, even though every single past rider ever had gained weight when they got home. It won't be a surprise to learn that my optimism was unfounded and that I piled on the pounds from the minute I set foot back in Blighty. I wanted to eat all the foods I hadn't had for a while. My body was still demanding 5000 calories a day, but I was no longer burning them up on the bike. How sad to realise I was just like everyone else and that the same rules applied.

That night we were camped in Ellands Bay, on a grassy cliff overlooking an endless stretch of white sand. I could hear the waves in my tent, and was tempted in to the water for a bit of frolicking in the surf. We hadn't been near a beach since the lake in Malawi and this was the sea. I think the seaside brings out the child in every one. I walked barefoot in the sand, had ice cream and collected shells and paddled. All the things that make you happy. In the camp, it was feeling festive with beers and a couple of folk playing their guitars.

This beach also provided the background for the TdA venture into erotic photography. A strange sentence to write, and an even stranger experience to participate in. After the success and hilarity of the naked mile, the idea had come up to do a Calendar Girls plus bikes and boys. I am not sure what this obsession with nakedness was all about. Can't say I shared it but I was certainly willing to be photographer – for the women – and to be amused and just a touch pervy about the boys.

Our first group was the racing boys. All of whom, I have to say, looked in great shape. They had chosen Kristian Pletten to take the shots. He was our semi-official tour photographer and had been taking great pictures the whole way down the continent. Luke, Dennis, Paul Spencer, Bastiaan and Scott stripped off, mounted up and thanks to some well synchronised pedalling and judiciously positioned thighs, got a perfect shot that didn't make you want to cover your eyes and scream.

My group of girls were more circumspect. We got up early and scampered down to a deserted cove, where they shed all the fleecy layers. It was really chilly, so I admired their bravery. As both artistic director and photographer, I had a whale of a time. Sand, waves, driftwood, seaweed all came into play at some point. The best shots, I thought, were the ones from the back though, with them running and jumping on the beach. I had to reshoot a couple of times. Camera shake due to uncontrollable giggles. Rosy cheeks all round.

I was looking forward to getting off the bike and resting my tired body, but I was dreading the TDA end and the beginning of reality. This day, though, reminded me that there were going to be lots of things back in Blighty to enjoy and re-connect with: Family, friends and shopping for a start.

We were now in Marelie's country and she had invited us to take a couple of detours. The first one was to meet her Aunty. We rode on a little faster, Carrie, Marelie and I to give us some time for a home visit. When we got to their house, a big family group was waiting to greet Marelie, a returning heroine, and her two grimy friends. Her Aunt, Cousin plus Wife and Granny were all there.

This was the first time I had been in someone's home, in fact in a real house, for months and it made me realise how feral I had become. We arrived filthy and soaking wet and even though we left our shoes and socks outside, I was hideously aware of the beautiful cream carpet.

The family couldn't have been more hospitable. They were so excited to see Marelie, and exclaimed over her cycling muscles, tan, wet clothing and skinniness. She immediately zoomed off to weigh herself and was very happy to have lost a few kilos on her long adventure. We were pressed down into comfy sofas and Aunty bustled into the kitchen, where very nice smells were emanating from. We were all a bit chilly, so the heating was put on – heating! What a luxury.

Aunty brought out a tray laden with cakes, tea and delicate tea cups and saucers and napkins. The tea was scalding hot and delicious and we were forced – no, really – to eat as much homemade cake as was humanly possible. Even better than the warmth, comfortable chairs and boundless cake, though, was the welcome and the feeling of being in a family. We couldn't stay for long unfortunately, as there were miles to do.

We got up to leave and Oh! the shame of it. We had all left big wet stains on the pristine sofas, where our sodden cycling bottoms had been.

Our next mini adventure of the day was a detour into Langebaan, Marelie's home town. This wasn't on our route and I felt like a criminal from deviating from the plan. Clearly, I was both feral and institutionalised. But the prospect of seafood, ice cream and a great clothes shop were too tempting and we struck off. We were spotted though, by Bastiaan and Liam, and their curiosity was aroused. They pedalled after us, and though we tried to outpace them, they soon caught up and off we all went to Langebaan.

Again, it was real life, seeing where Marelie came from and hearing her family stories as we ate lunch in her favourite cafe overlooking the beach. We wanted to go shopping, so the boys rode off back to the main route.

At the end of the trip, in Cape Town, there was going to be a big party for us, so Marelie and I both wanted to buy something gorgeous to wear.

"Don't worry, Alice, I know the best shop. You'll love it, we'll definitely find something," she had told me a couple of nights before when we were talking about the party.

She was so right. If you are ever in Langebaan, go to Miami Blue, and take your credit card. Mine got a bashing. It was another first. I had been buying things along the way, but this shop was like a proper clothes shop back home, and I went a bit wild. My dress for the party was a long, grey tube dress that tied on one shoulder and had fringes down one side. I loved it. It was called "Wow" dress on my receipt that contained eleven other items.... oops.

We stuffed our shopping bags into our backpacks and got back on the bikes. It was getting really late and I was a bit worried about getting back to camp. Marelie had the solution. She called her friend, Leon, and he turned up with his estate car. Bikes in the back, me squished in beside them and off we went.

We got him to drop us 5km from the end, so we could cycle in and no-one need ever know. I know, very bad, but we were near the end of the trip. Tent up, I took out all my new, shiny things and admired them.

It was our last night under canvas. Tomorrow, we were riding into Cape Town.

The cooking team, headed by Kim, had pulled out all the stops. We had had good food the whole way, with occasional highlights for birthdays, or of steak. This, though, was on a whole different level. The dishes just kept on coming. How do you cook lobster and mussels in cream and wine sauce for 70+ people on just a couple of burners? Something, that is forever to remain a mystery to me.

We had our final rider's briefing and the beers circulated. It got dark and in that weird way that happens with groups, we all started to move towards the beach. Bastiaan was going to burn his tent. A sacrifice to the cycling gods. I thought bitterly of my travails with my tent, and reflected that that was one thing I definitely would not miss.

On the beach, our head torches shone like huge glow worms. We were in a big circle, ready for our pagan ritual. Chief Druid, Bastiaan, moved into the middle ready for the tent sacrifice, Scott let loose a flaming arrow. It went up with a woosh of flame and sparks and we all danced around like crazy people.

What did it mean? I don't know. A way of letting off steam, a way to mark the end of something, a celebration of victory, a burning away of all the hurts and struggles and pain of the last months. An ending.

I went back to my tent and started my evening ritual: pyjamas on, a cup of Rooibos and a little biscuit or two, write my diary, get my bag ready for the next day, snuggle into my sleeping bag, head torch off.

Crash, bang, belch, snort. The tent shivered and shook alarmingly, and the zipper was whisked up to the top with extreme force as Paul Spencer, Chris, Stephen and Nick burst into my little sanctuary. Tent Invasion! They had been down at the local bar and wanted the party to keep going. It was like being attacked by a gang of Labrador puppies, they were all floppy and giggly and full of anecdotes about their evening.

And then it had finally arrived, the day I had actually been dreading but also longing for the past few weeks. The last day.

And, there, before I sling my leg over the bar for the last time and ease into my saddle, it is time to take a pause and reflect on what this adventure meant to me.

I had undertaken it with little preparation and no real knowledge of where it would take me and what it would be like. I had absolutely no inkling that it was going to be as hard as it was. I thought I would have more time, that four months would stretch on forever. But they didn't.

I felt like I was almost propelled out of my home and my old world and into the new unknown before I had time to really think about it. I signed up in the late Autumn and spent the time till Christmas focussing on other things. I had to find the best possible scenario for the people and the company I was leaving behind in the face of the Tory cuts. I had been running a development agency for the creative and digital sector in the Northwest of England which relied on government and European funding as well as private capital. When the Tories came into power, they said they were cutting Quangos and abolished our core funder, the Film Council. We could have survived that, but they then announced they were abolishing Regions.... strange but true. So, we would have had to look for our money from all the different municipalities and counties in the Northwest to continue. That would have been complicated by the rivalries between two great cities – being both pro-Liverpool and pro-Manchester was not going to be an option. Even with the great deal we managed to cut with DCMS (Department for Culture Media & Sport) to move the regional agencies into a new national structure, Creative England, and the prospect of five years' guaranteed funding, we had to completely change and that would mean that two-thirds of the team were going to lose their jobs, starting with the senior management. I didn't really have time to worry about Africa, because I was worrying about that. I made myself redundant first but whether that was a brave or a cowardly act is something I still think about. There were three of us at the most senior level, and at least one had to go. I wanted to, the other two wanted to stay, and my deputy was ready to take on the merger into Creative England, and did a brilliant job. But still.

I was fit and had been exercising well all year. I rode my mountain bike almost every weekend round the muddy, snowy, slippery ascents and descents of the Peak District with John Mongo and his band of merry men and women. My weight was nice and low which definitely helped, but I wasn't really in the kind of shape to go jaunting across a continent.

I also didn't know a thing about bike maintenance and let's face it that did not change, even with a continent to practise in. My friend, Dave, who built my bike, tried to explain things to me, like how the gears and chain work. It didn't mean anything, sorry Dave, but why one gear is light and another is heavy, remains one of life's great mysteries.

I was incredibly lucky to have Dave's support. He knew what I wanted when I did not and built me a bike that did me proud. Every little detail was attended to and his years in building bikes and working in the bike trade meant he could pre-empt problems I might have had, right down to the different kinds of spares he gave me to take.

All the practical things had to be dealt with as well. I had to find someone to take on my house and my cats, somewhere to put my car, a system for dealing with ongoing bills (my Mum) and all of the mundane ongoing tasks.

Mentally and emotionally, I was desperate for a change, but whether I was ready for what was to come is a moot point. I had always enjoyed my jobs and had spent the last nine years working hard, building up an organisation in the creative and digital sector. It had been a struggle from the very first week, when I received a death threat and an influential person, who had never even met me, tried to get me sacked. Who knew that film funding could create such craziness? Thankfully, neither succeeded and we went on to be very successful and win a good majority of the endless battles that had to be fought. Anyone who thinks that working in the public sector is easier than the private, think again. Internecine strife is the norm. Show a bunch of agencies a pot of funding and it is like watching sharks in a blood bath. It had been great, but it had been tough. Fulfilling in the sense that we were doing something beneficial and helpful to our region and industry, but personally, less fun than it could have been. It was good to give it up.

Saying goodbye to family and friends was hard at the very end, but wasn't something I found too difficult. I was brought up in lots of different places and went to boarding school at eleven, so I knew that the people who mattered would always be there. And it was only four months. And the internet is a wonderful thing. And everyone was really excited for me, especially my family who were super-supportive, so that helped a lot.

That was the sum of the me that set off from Hayfield, via Edinburgh to Cairo. Before I set off, I wondered if the person that came back from Cape Town would be very different.

The trip proved to me that an optimistic nature is the best type to have. Before I left, a friend who was thinking of doing it with me, listed all the potential hazards and difficulties ahead. Most of them, had never crossed my mind. They all happened over the next five months and it didn't matter. If I had spent time worrying about them, it would have been wasted.

Of course, it is wise to plan and I wish I had been fitter and chosen a better tent, but really the race was raced on the ground. Things happened daily and you had to deal with them as they came up. Unless you had a direct line to God, you couldn't predict what was coming next, but you knew that whatever it was, you had to keep on biking.

The moment is the most important thing. Enjoy it if the weather is nice and your legs feel good and you are riding with someone you like. Suffer through it if it is 51 degrees and your bottom is taking a trashing from the ruts. The moments passed for good or bad.

I was surprised at how much I enjoyed the physicality of the thing. Being governed by your body and its needs, rather than your head and its implausible demands, is very relaxing. I was also horrified by the physicality of some of it. Squeezing away at the long, finger-like saddle sore that had developed between my left thigh and groin until it exploded in a welter of blood and pus was a low point.

The journey reaffirmed my pride in being strong and resilient. I was not the fastest or the best or any of the "ests" but I did it and that sense of achievement is something that you take on with you. I was also proud to be a woman in that group, doing exactly the same distances and in the same conditions as the men.

My love affair with Africa deepened. Seeing it up close and personal was a privilege. I felt like we skimmed across the surface like those little flying fish you see from the boat. We never had enough time in a place to get to know it, or enough time with a person to get to know them. But, now when I see a news piece about how Chinese roads are transforming the continent, I can picture a specific road being built in a specific place and what changes that will mean.

Being outside for four months was one of the best things. You reconnect to nature in a completely different way when you are not surrounded by walls and buildings. I moan incessantly about my tent and the camping, but the actual sleeping outside, going for a midnight wee under the stars and then cycling off as the dawn broke was wonderful.

Feeling really hungry is another thing I rediscovered. Not hungry, because you are on a diet, but hungry because you need fuel for those legs to get you through the next few hours and you have used up every single thing in your body. And everybody knows that food tastes better when it is cooked outside, especially when it is steak and cake cooked by the TDA cook team.

We were free from every responsibility and care of everyday life. All we had to do was ride our bikes and put up and take down our tents. That was it. When you look at what most western people do in a day and how complicated and busy life is, to strip it down to three things is extraordinary. The mental space and time won by this simplification was something we all talked about. The TDA bubble where everything was straightforward.

Human beings are nice and good. I have always believed that to be basically true, although world events would teach me otherwise. We all arrived in Cairo as strangers with different backgrounds, personalities and expectations. Lots of Type As clustered together to ride from one end of Africa to the other. What you had done or been before, what house you had, car you drove, family you had, really didn't matter. For this trip we were all born again in a sense. We all had to forge ourselves within the context of our new tribe, find our little space, make our allegiances and be what we wanted to.

Before I left, I had thought that it would be Africa itself that would have the biggest effect on me. It did have a big effect, but it was the camaraderie and friendship of my fellow riders that meant the most to me. Sharing the journey we did with each other and the millions of tiny things that happened over those months created a spirit of true community.

What did I learn? Not how to change a tyre, that's for sure. I learnt not to look ahead too much but to focus your efforts on the next little bit. I learnt that everything changes all the time whether you want it to or not. I learnt that your body and your mind are inextricably linked and you need to take care of both. I learnt that freedom and time are worth more than almost anything else. And I understood that effort really does bring reward.

These grand musings, however, were far from my mind as I woke up to The Final Countdown. It was pancakes for breakfast and a new cycling shirt, because we had been given our TDA ones and we were all wearing them. If you have ever seen a bunch of cows galloping up a field for no reason whatsoever, you can picture us all on that last day. Skittish. Everyone was hyper or hung over or both. Things that had been our everyday routine were being done for the last time. I took my tent down and stuffed it into the locker and almost felt nostalgic.

Our day was being broken into two. The first part to lunch was just us and then at lunch we were going to be joined by lots of cyclists from Cape Town who were coming out in solidarity and celebration.

We had just 100 km to go. A mere bagatelle. The girls formed their own peloton and we rode fast over the first section, singing The Final Countdown loudly and badly. We had to have a final coke stop of course, and there were some rolling hills just to keep us in our place, but we soon got to the lunch stop on the beach.

It was fiesta time. There were balloons and leis (garlands) tied around the lunch truck and table which was heaving with food. All sorts of things that we hadn't seen for months. There was smoked salmon and wine and cheese and grapes and little party sausages. Of course, there was also plenty of cake to feed our ravening sweet tooths. We may all have been feeling emotional about the end of the trip but I didn't notice it ruining anyone's appetite.

We gathered for our group photos on the beach and then took hundreds of each other and ourselves. Everyone was grinning like a maniac, hugging and kissing as it began to really sink in that we were about to finish.

Lots of other riders were gathered to accompany us on our way. There were people flying flags, and some friends and relatives had driven to join us at lunch, so there were some very happy reunions. The ride took us closer and closer to Cape Town. Sadly, that old adage of accidents happening when you are nearly home came true and we had two broken bones that day. Linda broke her pelvis in a crash with another rider, and Paul Wolfe broke his foot slipping down the steps of the truck when he went to get his bag. He had just won the Tour D'Afrique!

As we got right into the city, a whole horde of skate boarders joined us, weaving in and out of the group. We had speeches in the main square, and then we headed up to the park for our final celebrations. The champagne bottles, that riders had stuffed into their back shirt pockets got breached and corks popped and fizzed.

By now, friends, family and significant others were arriving in force. I had someone come to meet me too. Jeanette, my friend Gary's mother, lived in South Africa and he had ordered her to be there at the end. There she was and it really was lovely to have someone from home.

Then it was here. Our final moment. The podium. We all assembled into our country groups and walked under our flags. Adam was our star with a second place in the race for Britain. Ruth and I walked arm in arm with smiles so big that my cheeks hurt.

The winners and the Every Fabulous Inchers got their medals and we all clapped as hard as we could. My name was called.

"Alice Morrison, Great Britain. "

I walked up and bent my head to receive my medal as the applause rippled round me. My heart was as full as it ever could be.

I had done it. 12,000 km. 10 countries. Cairo to Cape Town.

Appendix

The Bike

My bike expert was David Ward who is a general cycling God. He builds and designs bikes for a living, but also spoke to various journos and riders to make sure we got the best build for the trip. Our number one concern was reliability. There was a mechanic with us but we couldn't guarantee a bike shop with all the parts so everything had to be strong and easily fixable.

The frame was a steel 16" On One Inbred http://www.on-one.co.uk/ which is the best steel hard tail frame available. The obvious reason for choosing a steel frame is that if it breaks it can be fixed by anyone with a welder.

Built like a tank, Dave decided to get the FSA Orbit Extreme headset.

Wheels were Shimano XT hubs http://cycle.shimano-eu.com/ with Mavic 321 rims http://www.mavic.com/ and DT spokes with Nyloc brass nipples. Ian Bolton of CP Cycles http://www.cpcycles.com/ built the wheels and they also gave me a fantastic discount on gear. This is pretty well a bomb proof combination. The XT hubs are as reliable as you are going to get. The rims can handle anything you throw at them and the Nyloc nipples just don't come loose. Ian stretched and stressed the wheels as much as possible to avoid problems en route.

SRAM generously sorted me out with a whole bundle of great components. The rear Mec was a SRAM X9 nine speed for reliability and the shifters were also SRAM X9 http://www.sram.com. We also went for a SRAM chain and cassette matched up with a TruVativ Stylo chainset.
http://www.sram.com/truvativ

Forks took a bit of thinking about as we were going through wildly differing terrain from very long tarmac days to nasty corrugated and brutal lava flow. We wanted something highly adjustable, light and once again, reliable - step up RockShox SID Team http://www.sram.com/rockshox

I love my disc brakes but hyrdaulics could be compromised so we went for Avid BB7 http://www.sram.com/avid mechanical disc brakes with Avid FR5 brake levers.

Last but not least were the tyres. We could take three sets with us. Looking at the route we decided on two sets for road- Kojaks and

Schwalbe Marathon 1.6 http://www.schwalbe.co.uk/shop.sfxp and Racing Ralph 2.1 DD for the off road sections.

Image from Google Maps.

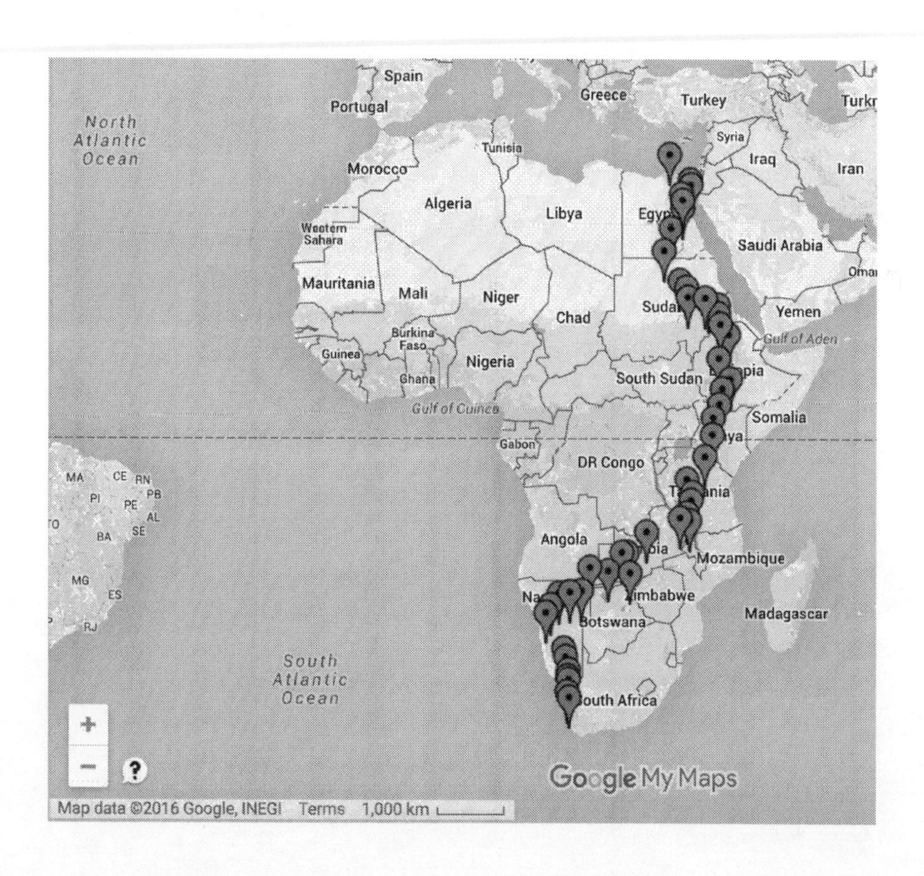

Acknowledgments

My very first thanks have to go to the TDA family. You made the adventure what it was and as I was writing this, I remembered each and every one of you with fondness and gratitude. I hope we meet and ride together again in the future.

Thank you to Mum and Dad for looking after all my finances and stuff while I was away and for being great cheerleaders

Thank you to Dave Ward for making my bike.

Thank you to my cousin, Charlie Mackenzie, for making my first website and helping with comms.

Thank you to Tanya Woolf for her editing.

Thank you to Scot Kinkade for his beautiful covers. I hope it is our first of many, Scot.

Thank you to Kristian Pletten for his photographs. http://www.kristianpletten.com/

Thank you to Cat Lewis for nagging me to write it.

Thank you to Karina for the initial inspiration by giving me a book about biking across Africa.

Thank you to Saira for the quotes and for trying to get me an agent.

Thank you to all of you who buy it and read it.

For more on me and my adventures www.alicemorrison.co.uk

For more on TDA and its adventures http://tdaglobalcycling.com

The End

If you'd like to see photos of the trip check out
www.alicemorrison.co.uk

Made in the USA
Middletown, DE
10 February 2021

33468953R00092